PUBLIC LIBRARIES

PUBLIC LIBRARIES

A TREATISE ON THEIR DESIGN,
CONSTRUCTION, AND FITTINGS

WITH A CHAPTER ON

THE PRINCIPLES OF PLANNING, AND A
SUMMARY OF THE LAW

BY

AMIAN L. CHAMPNEYS, B.A.
ARCHITECT

WITH MANY ILLUSTRATIONS OF MODERN
EXAMPLES AND FITTINGS FROM PHOTO-
GRAPHS AND DRAWINGS

𝔓𝔢𝔫𝔤𝔢 𝔓𝔲𝔟𝔩𝔦𝔠 𝔏𝔦𝔟𝔯𝔞𝔯𝔶.

CLASSIC EDITIONS

This edition digitally re-mastered and
published by JM Classic Editions © 2007
Original text © Amian L Champneys 1907

ISBN 978-1-905217-84-7

All rights reserved. No part of this book subject
to copyright may be reproduced in any form or
by any means without prior permission in writing
from the publisher.

CONTENTS.

	PAGE
CHAPTER I.—INTRODUCTORY AND GENERAL	1
CHAPTER II.—MATERIALS AND CONSTRUCTION	5
FLOORS	5
WALLS	7
ROOFS	8
STAIRCASES	8
DOORS	9
WINDOWS	10
CHAPTER III.—INSTALLATIONS AND APPARATUS	14
ARTIFICIAL LIGHTING	14
VENTILATION	21
HEATING	24
FIRE-PREVENTION	26
WATER SUPPLY	28
TELEPHONES AND SPEAKING-TUBES	28
LIFTS	28
CHAPTER IV.—SHELVING AND ACCESSORIES	30
MATERIALS	30
BOOKCASES:	31
DWARF CASES	38
STORAGE CASES	38
SHOW CASES	39
REVOLVING CASES	39
FOLIO CASES	39
STEPS, LADDERS, AND GALLERIES	40

CONTENTS.

	PAGE
CHAPTER V.—FITTINGS, FURNITURE, AND APPLIANCES	42
Materials	42
Cases for Maps and Prints	42
Exhibition Cases	43
Storage Cases for Files of Periodicals	43
Racks for Current Magazines and Periodicals	43
Directory-Stands	44
Reading Tables, Desks, and Easels	44
Newspaper Reading Slopes	48
Reading Room Chairs	50
Catalogue Fittings	51
Charging Appliances—	
Ledger Charging	53
Indicators	54
Card-Charging Appliances	56
Counters	57
Wickets	58
Partitions, Screens, and Barriers	59
Miscellaneous Fittings and Furniture	60
CHAPTER VI.—BOOK ROOMS	61
Stacks and Stack Rooms	64
Book Stores	67
Store-Rooms for Files of Periodicals	69
CHAPTER VII.—LENDING DEPARTMENT	70
Barrier System—	
General	70
Barrier System with Indicators	72
Barrier System without Indicators	74
Open Shelf System	76
Conclusion	80
CHAPTER VIII.—READING ROOMS	81
General	81
Reading Rooms for Periodicals	84
Newspaper Reading Rooms	84
Magazine Reading Rooms	87
General Periodical Reading Rooms	88

CONTENTS.

	PAGE
Women's Reading Rooms	88
Juvenile Reading Rooms	89
Other Reading Rooms	91

CHAPTER IX.—REFERENCE DEPARTMENT — 92

Barrier Reference Libraries	92
Open-Shelf Reference Libraries	95
Rooms for Special Subjects and Collections	97
Conclusion	98

CHAPTER X.—OTHER PUBLIC ROOMS AND SPACES — 99

General	99
Public Catalogue Rooms	99
Lecture Rooms	101
Spare Rooms	101
Public Lavatories and Closets	102
Refreshment Rooms	103
Bicycle Sheds	103
Public Entrances and Vestibules	103
Public Staircases	105

CHAPTER XI.—ADMINISTRATIVE ACCOMMODATION — 106

Workrooms	106
Cataloguing Rooms	107
Binderies	107
Receiving and Packing Rooms	107
Store-Rooms	108
Librarian's Room	108
Committee Rooms	109
Strong-Rooms	110
Mess-Rooms	110
Librarians' and Caretakers' Residences	110
Heating Chambers and Fuel Stores	111
Cleaners' Sinks and Cupboards	112
Waste-paper Bins	112
Entrances, Staircases, and Lavatories	113

CONTENTS.

	PAGE
CHAPTER XII.—FINANCE, ORGANISATION, AND BUILDING	114
INCOME AND EXPENDITURE	114
SITES AND DISTRIBUTION	117
SELECTION AND EMPLOYMENT OF ARCHITECT	119
CHAPTER XIII.—PRINCIPLES OF PUBLIC LIBRARY DESIGN	123
DISPOSITION OF DEPARTMENTS	123
ÆSTHETIC TREATMENT	135
CHAPTER XIV.—SINGLE LIBRARIES AND LIBRARY SYSTEMS	139
SINGLE LIBRARIES	139
LIBRARY SYSTEMS	144
CENTRAL LIBRARIES	147
BRANCH LIBRARIES	150
APPENDICES:—	
A. LIST OF ACTS OF PARLIAMENT RELATING TO PUBLIC LIBRARIES	155
SUMMARY OF PROVISIONS OF LIBRARIES ACTS	156
B. THE PUBLIC LIBRARIES ACT, 1892	157
THE PUBLIC LIBRARIES AMENDMENT ACT, 1893	173
INDEX	175

LIST OF ILLUSTRATIONS.

NOTE.—*In order that the comparative sizes of the libraries illustrated may be more easily comprehended, the whole of the plans of complete buildings are reproduced to a uniform scale of 32 feet to 1 inch.*

NUMBER.		PAGE
1.	Oak Sill in Wood-block Floor	6
2.	Plan of Revolving Door	9
3.	Standard Lamp on Reading Table, showing Arrangement of Wires	17
4.	A.—Rise and Fall Pendant. B.—Pendant with Cord Shortener. C.—Pendant arranged to suit altered Position of Tables	18
5.	Inverted Reflector used with Arc Lamp	19
6.	"Canting" or "Tilting" Pendant	20
7.	Rise and Fall Pendant for use in Book Stacks	20
8.	Diagram showing the Connection of Wires allowing a Lamp to be controlled from any of Three Positions	21
9.	Arrangement of Heating Pipes when carried under Shelving	25
10.	Wooden Bookcases	31
11.	Wooden Bookcase with Steel Stays	32
12.	Sections of Wooden Shelves	33
13.	Sections of Steel Shelves	33
14.	Bookcases with Projecting Plinth and Handles	34
15.	Tonks' Fittings	36
16.	Steel Bookcases	37
17.	Rolling Bookcases	39
18.	Folio Cases	40
19.	Swinging Step and Improved Grip	40
20.	Step Ladder	41
21.	Standard Rack for Magazines	43
22.	Rack for Time Tables	44
23.	Reading Tables with Plate-glass Tops	45
24, 25, 26A, & 26B.	Reading Tables	46, 47

LIST OF ILLUSTRATIONS.

NUMBER.		PAGE
27.	Reading Tables with Screen	47
28.	Single Table for Reference Readers	48
29.	Double Newspaper Slope	49
30.	Newspaper Wall Slope	50
31.	Slope for Seated Readers	51
32.	Standard Rack for Current Files of Newspapers	52
33.	Wall Rack for Current Files of Newspapers	52
34.	Card-Catalogue Cabinet with Sliding Runners	53
35.	Drawer of Card-Catalogue Shelves	53
36.	Sheaf Catalogue	54
37.	Cotgreave Indicator	54
38.	Chivers' Indicator	55
39.	Charging Tray	57
40.	Combined Book and Borrowers' Cards in Pocket	58
41.	Treadle Latch	59
42.	Book Room fitted with Wall and Floor Cases	61
43, 44, 45, & 46.	Arrangement of Bookcases and Windows in Book Rooms	62, 63
47.	Section of Book Stack with Five Tiers of Cases	65
48.	Section of Book Stack with Four Tiers of Cases	65
49 & 50.	Plans of Book Stores, showing Arrangement of Rolling Bookcases	67, 68
51.	Indicator Screen, Wakefield Public Library	72
52.	Lending Library Counter, showing Space left for Staff	73
53.	Delivery Desk, Massachusetts State Library	74
54.	Delivery Room, Milwaukee (Wis.) Public Library	75
55.	Staff Enclosure in Open Shelf Lending Library	76
56.	Staff Enclosure, Kettering Public Library	*facing page* 77
57.	Staff Enclosure to Lending Library, Kingston Public Library	77
58.	Plan showing Double Entrance to Open Shelf Lending Library	78
59 & 60.	Arrangements of Tables and Windows in Reading Rooms	82
61.	Newspaper Reading Room, Kettering Public Library	*facing page* 85
62.	Newspaper Reading Room, Kingston Public Library	86
63.	Reference and Reading Room, Carnegie Library, Homestead, U.S.	88
64.	Los Angeles (Cal.) Public Library	91
65.	State Historical Library, Madison, Wis.	94
66.	Reference Reading Room, Kettering Public Library	*facing page* 95
67.	Reference Reading Room, Kingston Public Library	95

LIST OF ILLUSTRATIONS.

NUMBER.		PAGE
68 & 69.	RYERSON PUBLIC LIBRARY, GRAND RAPIDS, MICH.	100
70 & 71.	DESIGN FOR CARNEGIE LIBRARY, OTTUMWA, IA.	125
72.	KINGSTON PUBLIC LIBRARY	127
73.	PUBLIC LIBRARY, WAYLAND, MASS.	128
74, 75, & 76.	CHELSEA PUBLIC LIBRARY	129
77 & 78.	ISLINGTON PUBLIC LIBRARY (NORTH BRANCH)	130
79.	WAKEFIELD PUBLIC LIBRARY	132
80 & 81.	CARNEGIE LIBRARY, PITTSBURG (HAZELWOOD BRANCH)	134
82.	CHELSEA PUBLIC LIBRARY	*facing page* 134
83.	ISLINGTON CENTRAL LIBRARY	,, 135
84.	BOSTON PUBLIC LIBRARY	,, 136
85.	REFERENCE READING ROOM, CHELSEA PUBLIC LIBRARY	138
86.	KINGSTON PUBLIC LIBRARY	*facing page* 138
87.	BIBLIOTHÈQUE STE GENEVIÈVE, PARIS	,, 139
88.	KETTERING PUBLIC LIBRARY	141
89, 90, 91, 92, & 93.	TYPES OF PUBLIC LIBRARY PLANS	143, 144
94 & 95.	ISLINGTON CENTRAL LIBRARY (FIRST PREMIATED DESIGN)	145
96.	ISLINGTON CENTRAL LIBRARY	146
97 & 98.	HACKNEY CENTRAL LIBRARY (SECOND PREMIATED DESIGN)	147, 148
99 & 100.	CARNEGIE LIBRARY, PITTSBURG (WEST END BRANCH)	149, 150
101.	BROCKLEY BRANCH LIBRARY	150
102.	LOWER SYDENHAM BRANCH LIBRARY	150

PUBLIC LIBRARIES.

Chapter I.

INTRODUCTORY AND GENERAL.

For the architect the spread of the public library movement throughout Great Britain and Ireland has lately added yet another to those special branches of his art with which he is nowadays expected to be conversant.

Nor, great as is the number of the library buildings which are already erected, is it likely that this field of architectural activity will have been exhausted within the immediate future, or that a knowledge of the principles of library design will become of less importance within the earlier half of the twentieth, than it has been in the latter part of the nineteenth century.

Nor, again, can it be reasonably affirmed that these principles have as yet been generally recognised or finally established. Since the present legal constitution of public libraries allows of no general co-ordination, any actual codification such as has been imposed upon the principles of school architecture is in their case impossible. Indeed, it is to be hoped that this constitution, such is its inadequacy in essence and in detail, may not prove permanent, and that therefore any step of such finality, were this otherwise considered desirable, would be at present premature.

Even within the limitations of the present system it is a fact that the existing examples of what a library building should not be are out of all proportion to those which are worthy to be followed. The greater number of the former are to be regarded as evidences of a necessary experimental process, while some are due to the vagaries of those local bodies upon whom the Public Libraries Acts now in force confer an irresponsible authority. It cannot, however, be denied that in many cases the architects are to blame, since they have sometimes wilfully sacrificed utilitarian to æsthetic considerations, and have only too often displayed a complete ignorance, or, what is worse, a very incomplete knowledge, of the special uses and requirements of this class of building.

Such failures, whatever their real causes, are apt to be imputed without discrimination to the architectural profession; and to this fact must be attributed the suggestion that librarians should dispense with the services of architects, and design their buildings for themselves.

Certainly the administrative organisation must be the key to the design, and with this the librarians are alone qualified to deal. It has indeed been objected that even here the difference of opinion that exists among librarians makes it impossible to accept their authority as final. The points, however, upon which they differ are the exception rather than the rule, and by the very fact of being still subjects of discussion are brought into somewhat undue prominence; nor can their existence in any way establish the claim of architects, or of others, to be considered competent arbiters on questions of library administration.

At the same time a knowledge of the ultimate requirements in no way implies a mastery of the structural means by which these may be attained; and that librarians are fitted by training or experience to deal with the latter is a proposition which no responsible man among them will for a moment defend, realising that the amateur in architecture is no less of an anomaly than the amateur librarian would be.

By all means let the librarian draught plans in order to develop his own ideas and afford suggestions to the architect, just as the latter may suggest modifications of the administrative system to meet the limitations of structural necessity; but the proper sphere of the one must remain the determination of the ends, and of the other the invention of the means.

The present work is intended primarily for the use of those who have either to prepare or to assess designs for library buildings; but it is hoped that it will be found helpful to library committees and others who may be engaged in the preparation of instructions for the architect.

In it no attempt is made to deal either with general principles of architecture or with those of library organisation, except in so far as each is affected by the other.

Again, though it is hoped that the subsequent chapters may demonstrate implicitly the requirements of library buildings generally, only those are fully considered that are constituted under the Acts relating to the British Isles. Even in those countries which have public libraries with a similar legal basis the detailed constitutions differ in so many particulars from those which obtain here that it is impossible to treat them as in any way homogeneous, though some few foreign examples, more especially of American libraries, which may be useful to British architects and librarians are adduced.

Moreover, in pursuance of the professed purpose of the book the history of the development of library planning will be ignored. The modern public library must be conducted on a principle essentially different from any of its predecessors.

In order to attain a maximum of efficiency within the limitations of a penny rate it must aim, as has been aptly said,* at becoming a "workshop" rather than a "museum." That is to say, indiscriminate book-collecting and book-preserving have no place in the organisation of a modern public library, and sentiment must be entirely sacrificed to utilitarian considerations. The librarian must aim at adding to his library only such literature as will be of practical use, and must not hesitate to discard such books as are out of date. The amount of literature which is of permanent general value is comparatively small, and the "lives" of nearly all scientific works, as of the majority of works of fiction, are of very few years' duration. It is not intended to imply that the question of selection and revision of stock is a simple one. This, however, is the business of the librarian, not of the architect. Its bearing, nevertheless, on the design is vital, since it makes it possible to fix a limit to the ultimate accommodation to be provided, and much modifies those considerations which are of such importance where the prospect of an indefinitely increasing stock must be remembered, but which have not infrequently imposed upon libraries a financial burden to which in their incipiency they have proved unequal.

As to the general order in which the subject has been treated, this may at first sight appear somewhat paradoxical. The following considerations, however, which have been the cause will also, it is hoped, be the excuse for its adoption.

As has been already said, the whole design of a library building must be the logical outcome of its administrative organisation, and therefore until the material, so to speak, with which this system has to deal is understood in detail, the conception of it as a whole must remain abstract and unconvincing. Consequently, in the subsequent chapters the fittings are first described, then the various rooms and spaces which contain them, and finally the complete library is shown as a working organism. In other words, though it is not suggested that an architect should construct the fittings and then build a library

---

* J. Duff Brown, "Manual of Library Economy," § 110.

round them, it is obvious that, unless he first knows what fittings each room is to contain and what rooms there are to be, he cannot form an idea of the requirements of the library in its entirety. As the fittings are consequent on the dimensions of the human body, so the rooms are dependent on the fittings, and the complete building on the rooms.

No doubt many arguments might be employed in favour of the reverse order of sequence, and the real defence for the choice of the present method is that it is thought that the matter will be in this way made more practically comprehensible, and therefore more useful, to the architectural reader, without becoming less so to others.

Chapter II.
MATERIALS AND CONSTRUCTION.

Though a knowledge of the potentialities and limitations of various building materials, and a mastery of the principles of sound construction and of the means of lighting, heating, and ventilating, form an essential part of the equipment of the library architect, they cannot be considered peculiar to this branch of the art, and will be dealt with only in so far as they affect or are affected by the special purpose and conditions of library building.

It may, however, be well to point out here that public library buildings are, as a rule, intended to be of a specially permanent nature, and, on account of their official standing, are usually thought worthy of a certain dignity and substantiality, while further they come under the category of public buildings as regards regulations and bye-laws.

The desirability of guarding as far as possible against the danger of fire is a consideration which to some extent affects the selection of materials. Absolutely fireproof construction, and the complete exclusion of combustible materials, would be, if not impossible owing to the cost, certainly impracticable for other reasons. It is obvious, however, that the risk from fire may be to a considerable extent reduced by various means, and these means will be dealt with under the subsequent headings.

Finally, as has been already indicated, economy, not only in respect of first cost but in view of the future maintenance of the fabric, must be a constant consideration.

Floors.—The chief requirements of the floors of library buildings are that they should be as far as possible incombustible, impervious to damp, noiseless, warm to the feet, and easily cleaned.

Solid floors are generally to be preferred throughout the building.

In the case of floors immediately below book rooms, many authorities recommend that there should be, if not a basement, at any rate an air-space beneath, in order to ensure absolute freedom from damp. In any case the whole site should, of course, be covered with a solid layer of cement concrete.

It has indeed been objected that the want of spring in solid floors renders their use tiring and injurious to the staff who have to stand and walk about on them for several hours at a time; but it seems doubtful whether such an objection is sufficiently real to counterbalance the advantages.

Wood-blocks, maple or oak rather than deal, are often recommended. They are warm and, except perhaps in those parts of the country where clogs are worn, sufficiently noiseless; while they can be easily kept clean.

It is important, if wood-block floors be used, that proper provision should be made where fittings are to be fixed to them. Barriers and similar fixtures when fastened to the blocks themselves are apt to loosen and pull them up. In such cases an oak sill, flush with the surface of the blocks, should be bedded in the concrete in order to afford a firm fixing (Fig. 1).

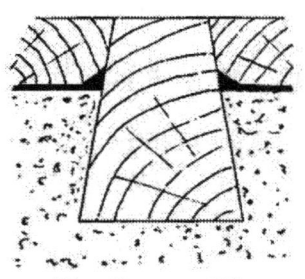

1. OAK SILL IN WOOD-BLOCK FLOOR.

Another form of flooring which has been used with advantage, and which is not only cheaper than wood-blocks, but in many ways preferable, is a floated cement surface on which is laid cork carpet, a material which is particularly warm and noiseless, and is very easily cleaned.

In rooms not used by the public, committee rooms and staff rooms for instance, special forms of flooring are not so necessary, and the same remark applies, to some extent, to lecture rooms, which are, of course, separated from the library rooms proper, and in which there is no continuous traffic. Moreover, for vestibules and corridors a more durable, and at the same time more ornate flooring, is often thought desirable, while warmth is a less important consideration. Marble or tile floors should not be used, since they are, if not too cold, certainly too noisy. Mosaic or some similar material is generally selected.

Where mosaic is employed it is well to avoid sharp contrasts of black and white, as these are rather apt to show the dirt and thus give the floor a slovenly appearance.

The plan sometimes recommended for hospitals and schools of making floors and walls meet in a curve instead of at an angle, in order

MATERIALS AND CONSTRUCTION.

to facilitate cleaning, is one which might with advantage be adopted in the public rooms and corridors of libraries.

The floors over public rooms should always be as far as possible sound-proof, and it is often desirable to make those over book stores waterproof. Various methods of ensuring both of these ends have been adopted. As a general rule, however, floors constructed with cement concrete are sufficiently proof against sound, and, certainly where pitch or "mastic," or better still asphalt, is used under wood-blocks, against damp also.

The soffits should be plastered and covered with a really washable distemper, or, where electric light is used, they may be painted.

Where floor coverings are necessary, carpets and fibrous matting of any sort must be avoided, since they harbour a large amount of dust. Linoleum, on the other hand, is rather cold and tiring to the feet, and, further, since it is apt to wear into holes where there is much traffic, continual renewals tend to make its use expensive, more especially if it is laid over the entire room. Thick rubber matting laid in the gangways is to be strongly recommended, while cork carpet, which has already been mentioned, has many advantages.

Walls.—Not only external but internal walls should be constructed as far as possible of incombustible materials. Hollow external walls are, more especially in exposed positions, conducive in many ways not only to the comfort and convenience of readers and staff, but to the welfare of the books.

Where a library abuts against another building great care must be taken to prevent the penetration of sound, especially where the adjoining premises be used for any particularly noisy business. If possible a space of two or three inches at least should be left between the outer wall of the library and that of the building next to it, and this space may be packed with some such material as silicate.

Partition walls, also, should be as far as possible sound-proof.

The internal faces of all walls in public rooms and spaces should, except where fittings are to be fixed against them, be lined to a height of not less than 6 ft., and for preference 7 ft. 6 in., with a dado of some washable material, usually wood, tiles, or glazed bricks. To some extent the tiles and glazed bricks are preferable, as being not only incombustible, but generally more sanitary; while tiles have some advantages over bricks, the joints being closer and fewer. Wood, however, has certainly the advantage in appearance, and, in positions which do not expose it to a great deal of wear and tear, it may be preferred to the more utilitarian but less comfortable tiles. Above the dado the walls should be plastered and coated with a washable paint or enamel.* All external angles in exposed positions should be rounded off, and, except where this would cause difficulties with fittings, the same might be done with the internal angles, as has been recommended for the junction between floor and walls.

Roofs.—The chief requirements of roofs are, of course, that they should exclude moisture, resist fire, and keep the building warm in the winter and cool in the summer.

With regard to the first of these, not only must thoroughly waterproof coverings be used, but in this country, where heavy falls of snow and subsequent thaws have to be taken into account, long gutters should be avoided.

As to safety from fire, where the building is so situated as to be liable to risks from conflagrations in adjoining premises, the covering should, of course, be incombustible. Frequently sparks and brands ignite the roof of a neighbouring building, and skylights are particularly dangerous in situations where such a contingency is possible.

It must also be remembered, more particularly in regard to eaves, cornices, and barge-boards, that frequent painting involves a considerable increase in the cost of maintenance, and consequently a large amount of woodwork in exposed positions should be avoided, not only on the ground of risk from fire, but on that of economy as well.

With regard to the internal treatment of roofs, as a general rule an open roof over a public room increases the difficulty of maintaining an equable temperature, and is not infrequently disadvantageous in respect of lighting and ventilation, and flat ceilings are therefore usually preferable.

Staircases.—The arrangements and dimensions of staircases in public libraries vary according to their position and use, and cannot therefore be dealt with in any general manner. It is, however, required by the London Building Act that "every staircase for the use of the public shall be supported and enclosed by brick walls not less than 9. in. thick"; that "the treads of each flight of stairs shall be of uniform width"; and again that "no staircase, internal corridor, or passage-way for the use of the public shall be less than 4 ft. 6 in. wide." This width, however, may be reduced to 3 ft. 6 in. in cases where not

---

* For colouring of walls see page 13.

MATERIALS AND CONSTRUCTION.

more than two hundred persons are to be accommodated. On the other hand, if the number of persons to be accommodated is more than four hundred, an additional 6 in. over and above the width of 4 ft. 6 in. is required for every additional hundred persons. The width, however, need never exceed 9 ft. If the staircase is 6 ft. wide or more, it must be divided by a central handrail. Two smaller staircases may be substituted, provided that each is at least two-thirds of the width prescribed for the single staircase, and provided also that neither is less than 3 ft. 6 in. wide. Similar rules apply to passages and corridors.

With regard to materials it is, of course, of the greatest importance that all staircases should be fireproof.

Most stones are liable to destruction under great heat, and this material is not therefore recommended. Stone steps also have the disadvantage of wearing down with use.

Concrete stairs are a good substitute, but should be covered with lead or wooden treads which can be renewed when worn, and which deaden the noise.

Granolithic, with lead dowells inserted to prevent slipping, may also be used, but its appearance is rather against it.

In America iron stairs are very popular. These, too, should be fitted with lead or rubber treads.

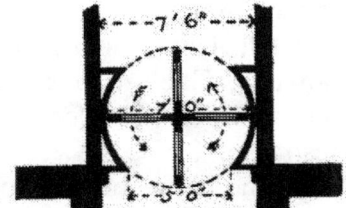

2. PLAN OF REVOLVING DOOR (USED AT KINGSTON AND WAKEFIELD PUBLIC LIBRARIES).

Were it not for the cost, perhaps the best form of all would be a solid staircase of hard wood.

Whatever material is used care must be taken that the nosings do not project too far over the risers, or there is a danger of tripping.

Doors.—As with staircases, so the arrangement and dimensions of doors must vary according to the particular circumstances and conditions, though the regulations for public buildings generally require that they shall open outward, and shall have no outside locks or bolts.

A few general considerations may, however, be noted :—

External doors which are kept open except during the hours when the library is closed to the public should be substantially made, and, generally, without glazed panels. They are usually double, and should be so arranged that they can be fastened open.

Inside these is usually an inner door or doors. Double swing-doors, or a revolving door (Fig. 2), which separates those entering from those leaving the building, and so prevents confusion, are generally used in such a position. Revolving doors have the great advantage of excluding draughts, and incidentally of checking the influx of dust.

Whatever form of door is used, it should be so made that it may be fastened open when desired for purposes of ventilation.

Sometimes turnstiles are employed for registering the number of those who use the library. These have the disadvantage of being very noisy, and should never be used unless they can be so placed as not to cause disturbance to readers.

Occasionally iron folding doors may be employed with advantage where a part of the building only is open at a time.

For public rooms double swing doors are usually considered best, though in some cases, as will be shown later, wickets may take their place; and sometimes, indeed, the entrances are left quite open.* Where this can be done without sacrificing the quiet and warmth of the rooms, or causing wastefulness in heating, it is often in many respects advantageous.

All swing doors in the building should, of course, have glazed panels. Each flap should be provided with a handle on one side, and a finger-plate on the other. Check-springs are altogether undesirable.

The name of the room should be legibly printed above the door, on one of the rails or on the glass.

Alternating swing doors, except where the opening is of necessity very narrow, should be avoided, as they are very liable to get out of order.

Owing to the width usually required, care should be taken that the openings are not of an unnecessary height or the weight of the flaps will be such as to lead to inconvenience, and perhaps to accidents. A height of 6 ft. 6 in. is sufficient, in nearly all cases, for the actual opening.

Windows.—Throughout a library building a plentiful admission of daylight and fresh air is necessary.

Except where light is obtained mainly from the roof the question of aspect is an important one.

While the direct rays of the sun are often sufficiently powerful to become an inconvenience to readers and a source of injury to books, yet such are their purifying properties, that their total exclusion is not recommended.

---

* *Vide* Fig. 73, p. 128.

MATERIALS AND CONSTRUCTION.

For this reason it is inadvisable that any of the rooms in a library, but more especially those to which the public are admitted, should be lighted exclusively from the north.

A west aspect, on the other hand, which admits the almost horizontal rays of the sun at a time of day when public libraries are often much frequented, should be as far as possible avoided.

Where possible, therefore, rooms should be lighted, partially at any rate, from the south or east.

With an east aspect the sun is to a large extent off the windows before its rays have attained their full power, and generally before the library is much used; while with a south aspect, the rays, at the time of year when their power is most considerable, fall at a steep angle and do not penetrate far into the room.

Blinds, made of some material which does not retain a quantity of dust, should be provided for all windows except perhaps those facing east and north.

They should generally, and with west aspects always, roll from the sill upwards. Indeed, it is often an advantage, especially with a south aspect, if two blinds are provided for each window, one rolling upwards, the other downwards, in order that the shade required in any part of the room at any particular moment may be secured with a minimum loss of light.

The arrangement of the blinds in each instance must, however, depend to a large extent upon the shape and size of the particular room and the disposition of the furniture and fittings.

Provided that due care is taken to regulate the admission of direct sunlight it is difficult to have too much window area in library rooms; for it must be remembered that the lighting area should be sufficient to allow of readers seeing small print not only on bright but on cloudy days, and this in the least well lighted parts of the rooms.

The relation of glass area to floor space in reading rooms must depend, of course, to a large extent upon surroundings and aspect, as well as on the relative positions of windows and fittings. The proportion should not, however, under the most favourable circumstances, be less than one to six, and one to four should be secured if possible.

The glass should be as near the outer face of the wall and carried up as close to the ceiling as possible; the openings being for preference square-topped. In the case of the class-rooms of schools the minimum height of the windows above the desks in relation to the depth of the room has been given as being in the proportion of two to five, and this rule, which may be safely applied to the reading rooms of libraries, should be remembered in determining the heights of rooms.

The height of the sills is another important consideration. Frequently it is fixed by that of fittings placed under the windows. For example, where newspaper reading slopes are placed beneath the windows, a height of 6 ft. is necessary in order that the sills may clear the tops of the stands. An additional 6 in., or better still 12 in., is however desirable in order that readers may not have the light too directly in their eyes. Sometimes, too, bookcases are placed against the wall immediately under the windows, in which case the height of the sills will depend upon that of the cases, which need not, of course, necessarily be of full height.

Where no such factor affects the height of the sills they should not, however, in the case of reading rooms at any rate, be lower than the height of the tables or desks, but generally slightly above these. A height of from 3 ft. 6 in. to 4 ft. or slightly more above the floor is usually satisfactory. Where such a height enables passers by to look into the building the lower panes may be fluted, stippled, or otherwise obscured. The raising of the sills solely in order to prevent those within from looking out is unnecessary; though in busy thoroughfares high sills are sometimes desirable for the purpose of ensuring quiet.

Where the sills are high care must be taken that they do not cast shadows on the nearest desks or tables, and if necessary they must be splayed. Often, too, it is desirable, for the same reason, to bevel the jambs and mullions: indeed, heavy mullions and transoms should always be avoided.

In many libraries various forms of metal windows have been used, but generally wooden double-hung sashes, if well and strongly made and easy to work, are to be recommended. It is also found extremely useful for purposes of ventilation if a top section of these be made in the form of a hopper, opening inwards and fitted with cheeks.

Generally speaking, as many windows as possible should be made to open, as there are times when the admission of too much fresh air would be impossible: and it is essential that all the windows should be readily accessible for purposes of cleaning.

Plate glass in large sheets is usually recommended for the windows of library buildings, but its æsthetic disabilities and the expense of replacing it in case of a breakage may be considered sufficient reasons for its exclusion.

Wooden sash-bars are preferable in many ways to lead cames: they should not, however, be too heavy nor the squares too small.

MATERIALS AND CONSTRUCTION.

Where rooms have to be lighted wholly or in part from narrow streets, wells, or areas, prismatic glass may be used with advantage.

Vertical windows in the walls are, generally speaking, preferred to top-lights. They give more facilities for ventilation, are less liable to admit water and to cause down-draughts, while roof-lights often make the rooms uncomfortably hot on sunny days. Further, as has been pointed out, they sometimes increase the danger of fire from neighbouring buildings; and in heavy rain or hail they are very noisy. On the other hand, not only is top-lighting often the only method available, but it is a fact that, where the disadvantages mentioned above can be circumvented, no light is more suitable for reading than that which comes from above. A top-light, too, has the not inconsiderable advantage of permitting almost any arrangement of the furniture in the rooms in which it is used. Consequently, many authorities strongly favour the use of top-lighting for reading rooms, and for workrooms requiring especially good lighting.

Lantern lights are, where practicable, in many respects a more satisfactory form than sloping skylights.

Where top-lights are used, great care must, of course, be taken, more especially in book rooms, to make them absolutely water-tight, and to provide proper condensation gutters and weeping-pipes. If they take the form of sloping skylights they should be covered with galvanised iron wire guards outside.

The down-draughts can be to some extent intercepted by means of ceiling lights. These should be frosted so that they will check and diffuse sunlight. They should be accessible for dusting, and the space above them should be well ventilated.

It is, of course, very often desirable and even necessary to provide fanlights over the doors to assist the window lighting, and usually these should be made to open in order that through-draughts may be obtained.

The diffusion of light may also be greatly assisted by the substitution of glazed screens * for solid internal walls.

A very important consideration connected with the question of lighting is the colouring of the walls and ceilings. The latter should, of course, be whitened, while for the walls, or at any rate for a tile or glazed brick dado such as has been recommended, some shade of green or green grey is the least trying to the eyes and absorbs very little light. Woodwork in dados or fittings should not be darker than necessary.

---

* See Chapter V., pp. 59, 60.

CHAPTER III.

INSTALLATIONS AND APPARATUS.

Artificial Lighting.—As the majority of the users of public libraries are engaged in their own business affairs during most of the daylight hours, at any rate throughout the winter, good artificial lighting is of fundamental importance to the utility of the building.

In country places where neither electricity nor coal gas can be obtained, petroleum lamps are the most obvious form of lighting. These should be of the "regenerative" type, and of a pattern which does not cast a shadow immediately beneath it.

Alcohol lamps with mantle burners are a second alternative.

Acetylene gas, though requiring an installation of pipes and a couple of generators, gives a much stronger light than petroleum in proportion to the amount of heat and vitiation of the atmosphere. The great disadvantages of acetylene are, the overpowering smell which attends any escape, however slight: the difficulty of locating and therefore of curing these very small leakages; and the great amount of soot which may be deposited everywhere in the event of the minute holes of a burner getting partly choked and the gas burning on unobserved.

When coal gas is used it must be remembered that the noxious products, viz., carbonic, sulphuric, and sulphurous acids, and the dry heat from the ordinary type of burner are extremely injurious, not only to readers and staff, but to the books. The light, too, is very yellow, and, in most country places, the pressure very unsteady. It should never be used without proper globes to eliminate the fatiguing flicker due to draughts, and governors at each burner to remove the effects of the rises of pressure, such as flaring and hissing flames, and the burning of an excess of gas with an actual diminution of light. In towns such rises of pressure generally occur about twice in twenty-four hours, and in country places more irregularly.

Incandescent gas burners give a much better light, because their illumination depends on the heating powers of the gas and not on what

INSTALLATIONS AND APPARATUS.

used to be called its illuminating power, which is often poor. Such burners are therefore primarily most economical. Owing to the extreme fragility of the mantles, the pendants, unless the ceiling is entirely free from vibration, should be fitted with spiral springs. It is also recommended that there should be a contract with the makers or fitters for their maintenance and for the cleaning of the lamps. The inverted pattern is attractive by reason of its advantages, notably the absence of shadow, which gives a very satisfactory light for reading. It has, however, the disadvantage of "burning back" under certain conditions of draughts. This burning back, when once it occurs, generally burns the lacquer off the fitting in question, and often so heats the metal work as to crack the glass or porcelain parts associated with it.

For the general lighting of rooms where coal gas is used, the "ventilating multiple incandescent" mantle burner of high power is desirable, since the products of combustion are carried away immediately. This may be used with inverted reflectors (see Fig. 5, p. 19), a method which will be further discussed below. Its free use is somewhat limited by the unsightliness of the long runs of large ventilating pipes, but in high positions these tubes easily pass unnoticed.

On the whole, the best method of lighting a library is by electric light. In very large libraries this may be specially generated, and it has been found, in institutions where the demand for light is somewhat similar (in point of time of consumption) to that of a library, that town gas can be used in gas engines to produce electric light more cheaply as regards running expenses than by consuming the gas direct in gas burners.

Where this is done, in order to use machinery of the smallest size compatible with efficient lighting, it is well to employ accumulators, and to charge these slowly throughout the day so that they are ready for the heavy demand which comes upon them each evening. In the absence of accumulators the plant must be large enough in engine power to cope with the maximum demand, engines must be duplicated to provide a complete stand-by against breakdown, and the large double plant so installed stands (like so much locked up and uninvested capital) idle throughout the long hours of the day.

When current is bought by meter from a public supply company, it will be noted that the price charged per unit depends upon a certain sliding scale which varies in different localities. For example :—

Current for Lighting	- - - -	6d. per unit.
,, Basement Lighting	- - -	3d. ,,
,, Power Purposes	- - -	2d. ,,
,, Heating Purposes	- - -	1d. ,,

The exact meaning of these terms is perhaps worth looking into. The lower rate for "basement lighting" can generally, by negotiation with the supply company, be extended to include any lights placed in rooms which cannot obtain sufficient daylight at any time to allow artificial lighting to be dispensed with in daylight hours. Such lamps must, however, be wired to the special "basement" meter, otherwise no reduction of charge can be obtained. Lights in dark parts of a basement all come under this category, and as it is to the supply company's interest to induce the user to employ electric light during the daylight hours, the company's officials will be very willing to consider favourably a reasonable extension of the term "basement" which may secure them from any introduction of coal gas to the "long hour" lamps.

The low cost of basement lighting is a consideration which may often be with advantage taken into account in the disposal of book stores and such rooms as are little frequented, more especially where a library has to be planned on a site where the possibility of obtaining good window-lighting is limited.

The still lower rate of 2d. per unit for power purposes has caused some keen librarians to consider whether it would not pay them to take current for a motor which should itself drive a dynamo powerful enough to light the building through the intermediary of accumulators. The inducement to introduce this amplification is the difference in price between 6d. and 2d. per unit.

It is just possible that if a small motor and dynamo were kept running day and night charging a battery of accumulators, the supply company might not only *not* object to, but actually welcome such a method of storing their product when cheap, and using it when dear. But whatever may be done in particular cases, the principle is one to which the supply company is sure to be strongly opposed, because it is so very liable to be abused.

A grave abuse would be exemplified by the case of a librarian who might employ a motor and dynamo of the full size of his lighting demand *and with no accumulators*. Such a person would take his full load current at the ordinary lighting up hours of the town, and would not draw current when it is cheap, *i.e.*, in the daylight hours and small hours of the morning. He would, however, be paying a cheap rate, and would be defrauding the company. This, at all events, is assuredly the view the company would take, and the matter is worth so much money to the company that there is little doubt the question would be fought at law, and, if need be, taken to the Court of Appeal. Even if the united supply companies failed on appeal, an Act of Parliament would be sure to put them right eventually, so that the purchaser of the motor-dynamo combination would have paid dearly for his experiment in economy.

The tempting price of 1d. per unit for heating, good as it is, is too expensive for the warming of large rooms, or even small rooms which are so used as to require any appreciable amount of ventilation. A small radiator under a knee-hole desk taking current at the rate of about a halfpenny per hour may, however, be a very valuable, comfortable and not unduly expensive appliance for the use of favoured individuals—the chief librarian, for example.

The advantages of the electric light are that it heats the air only to a very slight degree, and vitiates it not at all; while the danger of fire, if a proper sub-fuseboard system is employed and properly carried out, is less than with any other method. The extra cost is to a great extent balanced by the resultant economy in depreciation of leather and cloth bindings, in cleaning, sick-leave, insurance, and re-decoration.

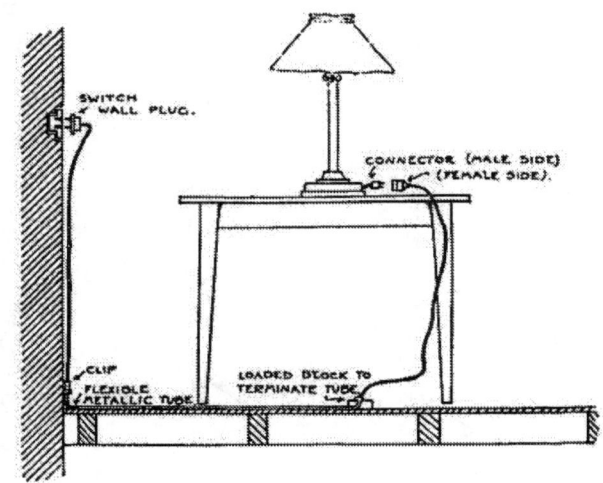

3. STANDARD LAMP ON READING TABLE, SHOWING ARRANGEMENT OF WIRES.

Whatever form of lighting is adopted the choice of the power and the disposition of the lamps will largely determine both the comfort and economy in use. The positions should, of course, be determined by the disposition of the furniture and fittings, and not primarily by considerations of symmetry or architectural effect.

For library reading, more especially where readers may wish to take notes or make copies, the strongest light should, as far as possible, come to each individual over his left shoulder. At the same time, it is most important that the whole room should be well lighted, since isolated points of light in a dark room are very trying to most people, owing to the dilatation and contraction of the pupil which takes place each time the eyes may glance up from the well-illumined paper to the dark surroundings and back to the paper again.

When the height of the room is not very great lamps about 8 ft. or 8 ft. 6 in. above the floor are recommended. Where the ceiling is high it is usually best to provide lighting on two levels, viz.—(*a*) *below:* frequent small standard lamps with proper shades at a height of 2 or 3 ft. above the tops of the tables or desks (Fig. 3), or "rise and fall" pendants (Fig. 4, A), or pendants with cord shorteners (Fig. 4, B); and (*b*) *in the upper part of the hall:* a few arc lamps of the "Union" or other similar type at such a height as to secure a good diffusion of light over the whole room from the ceiling and walls. As has already been indicated, the light obtained from inverted reflectors (Fig. 5) is very desirable in large reading rooms, and, where the extra expense can be

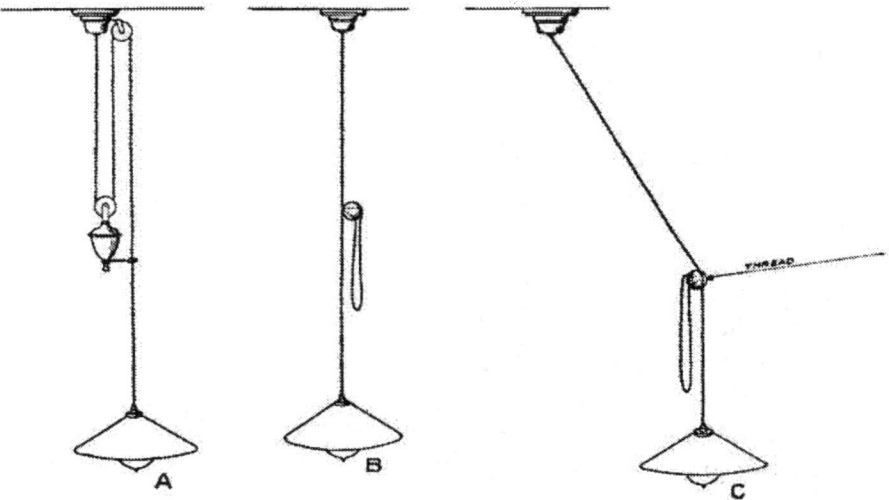

4. A—Rise and Fall Pendant. B—Pendant with Cord Shortener. C—Pendant arranged to suit Altered Position of Tables.

faced, these are strongly to be recommended. A flat white ceiling and a light-coloured cornice and frieze are, of course, a great assistance to such general lighting.

Whether pendants or standards are preferable for the lower lights is a matter for individual preference. Certainly pendants have the advantage of leaving the whole of the table surface free, and if the somewhat unsightly appearance of the flexibles which suspend them is ignored they can be fastened in different positions if a rearrangement of the tables is desired (Fig. 4, c).

It must, of course, be remembered that the area of the retina affected by the fine filament of the electric lamps is very small, and the intensity therefore great, so that, where the filament can be seen, diffusion should be assisted by the provision of suitable globes and shades, while the lamps must not be of too low a power, nor too widely distributed. For reading lamps 12-in. opal and green or double shades are recommended.

Lamp bulbs which have been frosted have the effect of giving a much larger luminous area than the plain filament, but they waste about 25 per cent. of the light in so doing. Tantalum lamps, owing to the very great length of the filament, give an impression of a large luminous area, and are exceedingly economical in current. Their drawback is their cost of 3s. as against 1s. for ordinary carbon filament lamps. When, however, current is expensive and the voltage under 120 volts, the net gain is considerable.

If frosted lamps are used at all, the lower part, *i.e.*, the part which meets the eye, should alone be so treated. Half-frosted lamps are now commonly in the market.

Holophane globes are economical for use in corridors and passages, but should not be used for the reading tables.

With regard to the distribution of the lights, 16 candle-power lamps should be so arranged that no reader will be more than 6 ft. distant from the nearest.

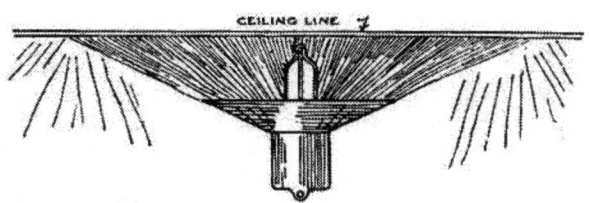

5. INVERTED REFLECTOR USED WITH ARC LAMP.

Where standard reading lamps are provided on the tables they are usually connected with sunk floor plugs placed close to one leg of each table; an alternative which allows of tables being moved about on a limited radius is shown in Fig. 3. This plan allows easy control of the switch plug, and removes the plug from the danger of being wetted when the floor is washed.

The wires are either twisted round the table legs, or taken up in grooves.

The chief objection to floor plugs is that they are apt to fix too rigidly the positions of the tables, and render any rearrangement of the furniture difficult. It would seem, however, that, provided the flexible wires do not cross the gangways, but lie under the tables only, there would be no great objection to their lying loose on the floor. In case this were to cause difficulty in respect of insurance a large-sized wall plug could be fixed in the floor under a cupped and screwed or hinged board.

Newspaper reading slopes may either be lighted by pendants or by brackets fixed to the slopes themselves (see Figs. 61 and 62).

For bookcases tilting pendants with reflectors (Fig. 6) are recommended.

In book stacks, where there is only just head-room between the decks, small bulbs at frequent intervals are fixed to the soffit of each deck. Perhaps a better fitting would be a "rise and fall" pendant with a protected lamp hooked to a taut phosphor bronze wire along which it can be pulled backwards or forwards as desired. These wires would, of course, be close to the soffit of each deck, running lengthwise along the gangways between the bookcases (Fig. 7).

Hand bulbs are never satisfactory.

The arrangement of the switches in a library building is important. Where rooms are provided with lights at two levels as recommended above, the most economical arrangement is that by which each of the lower lights over any particular table or desk is governed either by a switch lamp-holder or a wall-switch conveniently placed near the table in question, in addition to those wall-switches which control groups of lamps.

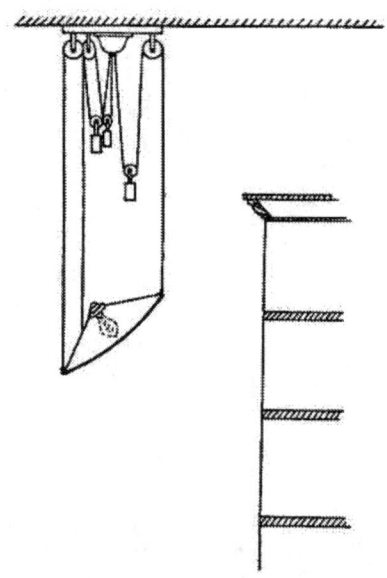

6. "Canting" or "Tilting" Pendant, which can be turned to throw light in any direction, and can also rise and fall.

In barrier lending libraries the lamps lighting the bookcases should also be separately governed, the switches being often placed on the ends of the cases.

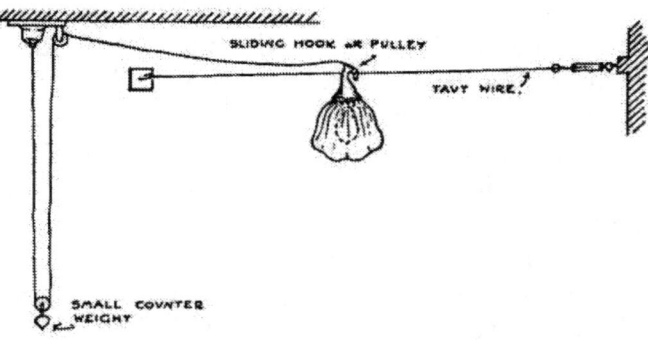

7. Rise and Fall Pendant for use in Book Stacks.

In open shelf lending libraries all the lights are usually kept on during the hours it is open, though in this and all other rooms of any size it is always best to have one or two lights which can be turned on

INSTALLATIONS AND APPARATUS.

separately for purposes of cleaning. Where there are two doors to the room, these may be controlled by two-way switches, so that from whichever door the room be entered the light can be turned on and the same light turned off, on leaving, at the other door.

An ingenious arrangement of switches for stacks with glazed or perforated decks is one which allows the light immediately above or below to be turned on from a convenient point in any story, so that the light on the top or bottom shelves of that story can be supplemented as desired. This is effected by two-way switches and "intermediate" switches and three-switch wires (Fig. 8).

Although where gas is used the taps should be so arranged that they cannot be turned off or on except by the staff, in the case of electric switches it is usually preferable to avoid the troublesome use of removable keys (which generally results in a waste of light) by placing all switches in conspicuous positions about 6 ft. 6 in. above the floor, where any interference can be easily seen by those in charge. Standard lamps, where used, are either provided with separate switches or each is controlled from its own wall plug as in Fig. 3.

8. Diagram showing the Connection of Wires allowing a Lamp to be controlled from any of Three Positions.

In large libraries a few petroleum, or better still colza, safety lamps should be kept lighted, in corridors and staircases particularly, to prevent absolute darkness in case of a failure of the regular system from fire or any other cause.

Ventilation.—Though thorough ventilation is essential to the welfare of readers, staff, and books, the atmosphere of public libraries in general, and of newspaper reading rooms in particular, has become a proverb, and will in all probability continue in this evil notoriety so long as the news-room continues to afford a free and agreeable shelter to the unwashed.

The essential condition of fresh air is space; but even if the limited incomes of our public libraries allowed of a liberal space being provided for every serious reader, they could hardly cope with the crowds of malodorous idlers who are only too ready to occupy the chairs and detain the papers in the reading rooms. Consequently, until these can be kept outside, the ventilating engineer cannot hope to do more than lessen the evil.

This evil is certainly much aggravated by packing the greatest possible number of seats into the smallest possible space; but on the other hand it cannot be recommended that the uncleanliness of unclean individuals should be taken into the calculation, a course which would necessitate the provision of areas similar to those required in hospitals.

The remedy is rather to exclude as far as possible the undesirables, and to allow a reasonably liberal spacing.

From 16 to 18 sq. ft. per reader is a usual allowance, but the latter figure ought to be regarded as the minimum. Indeed 20 or even 24 sq. ft. cannot be considered wasteful.

The height of the rooms is, of course, an important consideration in connection with this question. It is generally agreed that, as far as the needs of ventilation are concerned, a height of 13 or 14 ft. is sufficient, though of course in very large rooms a lofty ceiling is often required for the sake of appearance or in order to give the necessary height for the windows. Generally from 14 ft. to 16 ft. for large, and from 10 ft. to 12 ft. for small rooms is recommended.

Where a roof is ceiled at the collar, the heights should be calculated to give the same cubic capacity as if the room had a flat ceiling of such a height as that above indicated.

Liberality in respect of space and freedom from obstruction are, however, only necessary conditions of and not substitutes for actual ventilation.

Open windows are, of course, the most effective means, and, as has been recommended above, as many windows as possible should be made to open, while through-draughts should be secured where possible by means of fanlights.

In cold or inclement weather some system of artificial ventilation becomes necessary.

Unfortunately although this item should receive careful attention and the fullest scope should be given for securing a well-designed system, the authorities are generally most anxious to curtail as far as possible the expenditure in this direction. Consequently it is only too often that a makeshift system is adopted with a fervent hope that it will pass muster and that no complaints will be made by the subsequent occupants of the building. Engineers are, however, moving in the right direction, and the authorities are realising that this subject demands the fullest consideration.

It is now generally taken for granted that during cold weather the ventilating installation must be worked in conjunction with the heating. With radiators or pipes placed round the rooms below windows, and next outer walls, it is often somewhat difficult in large rooms to change the air in the central parts, more especially as in many cases such fixtures as newspaper slopes and double bookcases serve to check the air currents even where the air is forced by means of a fan or blower from one ventilator and exhausted by another.

Wherever possible, when large rooms are to be warmed and ventilated, it is an advantage to have one or more radiators fixed in the middle of the room as well as round the outer walls, and ducts should be formed in the floors to convey the air from the outside to the radiators. These will greatly assist in keeping the air throughout in motion.

Tobin tubes are no doubt of some use, especially during the summer, for introducing fresh air into the rooms, more particularly if the windows will not permit of a good through-draught, but they are generally considered rather objectionable during the winter by those sitting in close proximity to them.

Generally speaking, the conditions and requirements of a library in respect of artificial ventilation do not differ materially from those of other public buildings which are at times full of people. Consequently there is no need to discuss the many rival systems, for whichever of these is ultimately proved most efficient, will be the most suitable for a public library.

Care must, of course, be taken that the inlets are sufficient in proportion to the outlets, and that the former are so placed that the incoming air is warmed by radiators or pipes, both of which precautions have in some instances been notably neglected. In some cases, indeed, it has been found necessary to filter and wash the air before it enters the building, but this is seldom required in the case of municipal libraries.

Finally, whatever system is adopted, it should be calculated to give a change of air in all rooms not less than three to four times an hour, and in the average news-room a change six times in the hour would not be too much when the situation of the library is one where the air is especially impure or where uncleanly persons are admitted to the rooms. In such a case the use of the Plenum system would probably be advantageous, even if the other rooms were ventilated on some different principle.

There are, of course, many different types of extractors for removing the vitiated air, and when the building is well situated in country towns, and not surrounded by higher buildings, no doubt the automatic ventilators are suitable, but where the opposite is the case, mechanical or electrical extractors are certainly the best.

It is, of course, desirable to arrange the exhaust fans where they cannot be tampered with by the public, but are easy of access for the attendant. They must be absolutely noiseless, if connected by ducts to the various rooms, and must be protected from the weather.

A small ventilating fan such as is often seen fixed in a window is of very little use unless protected in some way from the direct force of the wind. Often this is of sufficient power not only to stop the fan entirely, but to reverse its running, making it an intake instead of an exhaust fan.

Wherever possible, flues should be built in the walls and carried up to the roof space, where the fan or other apparatus for exhausting the air should be fixed, and a turret or gablet formed through which the air can be discharged.

Heating.—It is important, in order to prevent discomfort from cold, during the winter months particularly, that public libraries should be provided with some system of artificial warming. In this country a temperature of from 60 to 62 degrees Fahr. is most suitable in the rooms; while for corridors, vestibules, and lavatories 56 degrees Fahr. may be considered sufficient.

It is most important, not only for readers and staff, but also for the books, that the heat should be well distributed.

The ordinary open fires[*] should be avoided not only in the neighbourhood of books, but in all public rooms; though they may be used in a librarian's room or committee room. The disadvantages of open fires are the unequal distribution of heat, and consequent wastefulness; the dust and noise which accompany the carrying to and fro of fuel and

---

[*] Open grates are much used in American libraries with wood fires, but they are, of course, intended chiefly for ornament, and at most are merely supplementary to an independent system of heating.

ashes; the time and labour spent in attendance; and lastly, their attraction for idlers.

Stoves, generally speaking, overheat the air and are injurious to books, but as they are very economical and free from most of the disadvantages of open fires they are often used in librarian's, committee, and staff rooms. Electric radiators are too expensive for use except to a very limited extent (see page 17).

Owing to the humid atmosphere of our English climate, heating by means of steam and hot air appliances is not very suitable unless great care is taken to distribute the heating surface or hot air inlets over as large an area as possible, and so reduce the temperature as well as the velocity of the air currents. When confined to small areas the high temperature and velocity are very objectionable and deleterious to books.

Particles of dust are attracted, carried along, and deposited on the nearest cold surface, while the absorbing power of the heated air dries the bindings of the books, and causes them to crack and crumble away.

High-pressure hot water also has the great disadvantage of the danger of bursts from obstructions in the small pipes, which are particularly subject to the attacks of frost.

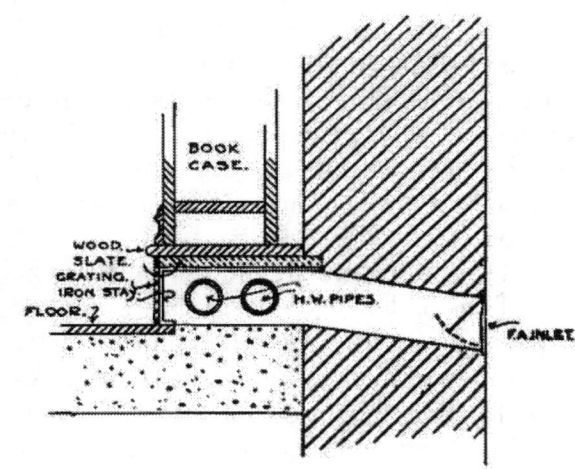

9. Arrangement of Heating Pipes when carried under Shelving.

On the whole, low-pressure hot water is the most economical, safe, and easily regulated system.

Distributing pipes should be carried in troughs covered in and packed.

No pipes or radiators should be placed near books. Occasionally it is impossible to avoid carrying pipes under the shelving, and when this is done they should always be covered by a slate slab, while there should be a board below the books projecting in front of the face of the shelving (Fig. 9).

Pipes distribute the heat somewhat more impartially than radiators and are cheaper, but the position of the fittings often renders their use impossible. Where they are adopted they should never be carried under gratings in the floor. By such an arrangement a large proportion of their heat is wasted, they are inaccessible for cleaning, and send up air-currents charged with dust. The proper method is to carry them on brackets round the walls so that they may be wiped every day with a wet cloth. They must, of course, be painted or enamelled or this process will cause them to rust.

Radiators are, as has been indicated, generally, and particularly in book rooms, more practicable than pipes. Their distribution should be carefully considered in relation to fittings and furniture, and to the system of ventilation: that is to say, they should not be placed where their heat will be injurious to books or uncomfortable for readers or attendants; while they should, where possible, be near doors and windows, and connected with the fresh air inlets.

Whether pipes or radiators be used, every facility must be given for regulating the temperature, more especially in the case of stacks with open decks, which are usually heated by radiators at the lowest level, and where the danger of overheating the books in the topmost tier is considerable. Automatic control by means of thermostatic valves is a great convenience where the funds are sufficient to meet the cost.

Thermometers should be fixed in each room.

The boiler, except in large buildings, should be a simple one, requiring only intermittent attention.

An automatic damper regulation for controlling the consumption of fuel is recommended for institutions of any considerable size.

The requirements of heating chambers and fuel stores will be considered below (Chapter XI.).

Fire-Prevention.—Notwithstanding the fact that books do not burn easily, so much damage and destruction has in the past resulted from the collapse of burning libraries that the need of precautions against fire has been much emphasised.

As regards construction and materials, the absolute fireproofing of the building would, as has been indicated, involve an outlay usually beyond the limit of the funds available, and consequently the library architect must aim rather at the elimination of all highly inflammable materials from the fabric generally, and from such structural parts as floors, walls, roofs, and staircases in particular.

In the main, however, safety from fire is to be sought, on the one hand in the selection of the site, on the other in the disposition of the building itself. These questions will be more fully treated in a subsequent chapter, but a few considerations affecting the matter may be dealt with here.

It is sometimes, especially in towns, impossible to obtain a site sufficiently detached from such buildings as are liable to originate a conflagration. In such cases the roof, more particularly if there be skylights in it, is usually the most vulnerable part, and should be especially protected. For this purpose drenchers may be recommended, though an additional precaution may be taken by using fire-resisting glass.

Where, on the other hand, immunity from dangerous neighbours can be secured, this sometimes involves an isolation which renders the building subject to risks from lightning. In such cases the provision and maintenance of an adequate and carefully planned system of conductors is important. Where a large amount of iron construction is used within the building, a steel book stack for instance, an external conductor would, of course, be useless. In such cases the steel construction itself should be utilised for this purpose, being connected in a suitable manner on the one hand with the terminals, on the other with ground-wires and earth-plates.

With regard to the disposition of the building, it is sometimes possible, especially in large libraries, to detach from the rest such departments as are most likely to originate a fire: for example, a heating-chamber or caretaker's residence; or else to isolate to some extent those parts in which the books are stored, an arrangement which, as has been said, will be further discussed below. As a rule, however, so long as a slow-burning construction is ensured, such a measure may be considered unnecessary, as may the provision of double fireproof doors, by means of which the book stores can be entirely shut off from the rest of the building.

In the average public library it is sufficient to provide a fireproof strong-room, or even a safe, in which records and possibly books of exceptional value may be kept; though it is sometimes recommended that all records and duplicate accession catalogues should be kept elsewhere.

Some sort of fire-extinguishing apparatus should, however, always be provided. Fire-hydrants and other appliances are often fitted up in libraries, but the opinion of most librarians would seem to be in favour of the ordinary fire-buckets, for preference those with rounded bottoms.

Indeed, when, as should always be the case, the staff is regularly drilled, buckets are scarcely less efficacious than the more complex devices, and cannot get out of order.

A plentiful supply of water both within the building and without should, of course, be available; and safety lamps should, as has been said, be provided in large institutions.

Water Supply.—A consideration somewhat closely connected with the prevention and extinction of fire is that of the supply of water. Besides the supply necessary in case of fire, water is required on each floor for cleaning. It must be remembered that water is hardly less injurious to books than fire, and therefore the greatest care must be taken that all water brought into the building shall be prevented from reaching the books in case of a leakage. The most frequent cause of such leakages is frost, and the pipes should consequently be well packed, and where possible so arranged that they can be emptied for the night at the bottom of the building. Sometimes, as a safeguard against this danger of leakages, the horizontal pipes are carried along in conduits lined with lead, and so arranged as to carry off immediately any water which may escape; while in some cases special waterproof floorings have been provided.

Telephones and Speaking-Tubes.—When possible every public library should be connected by telephone with the municipal offices, and each branch with its central. The central should also be connected with the exchange, unless a wire to the switch-board of the municipal offices is sufficient, in which case a great economy [*] can be effected. For communication between the different departments of the building speaking-tubes are generally perhaps to be preferred as simpler and less liable to disorders; though where these have been omitted in the first instance it is usually easier subsequently to instal the telephone. Moreover in very large libraries the telephone has the advantage that by means of a central switch-board a complete intercommunication can be easily established such as would involve a large number of independent speaking-tubes.

Lifts.—Small, quick-running lifts are often needed in public libraries for conveying books from one floor to another.

For these electro-motors are strongly recommended, particularly when used in connection with reading rooms, as they are noiseless and can be placed in odd corners out of the way.

The cages should be lined with leather or indiarubber to protect

---

[*] Mr J. Duff Brown says that the cost is about one-fourth that of the regular exchange service. "Manual of Library Economy," § 169.

bindings, and a small clip for carrying paper slips with messages or applications is sometimes attached.

Where there is an unpacking room, unless this is on the entrance level, it is a good thing to provide a lift capable of carrying heavy cases of books.

Passenger lifts may be required in very large libraries where the public accommodation is on more than one floor. Where a large reading room is placed at a high level such lifts are most necessary. They may also be used with advantage in high book stacks.

Chapter IV.

SHELVING AND ACCESSORIES.

Materials.—Though steel has to some extent taken its place, wood is still, in this country at any rate, the material most frequently used in the construction of bookcases.

Oak, walnut, and mahogany are generally considered the most satisfactory woods for the purpose. Teak has many disadvantages.

On the whole the best alike for æsthetic and utilitarian reasons, is oak. Owing to the cost, however, the use of oak is generally confined to such shelving as is within sight of the public; and even then the less exposed parts of the cases are often made of a different wood.

As a substitute for oak in the less visible parts of the cases, Archangel yellow deal is recommended.

The treatment of the woodwork of bookcases, and indeed of all wooden fittings in public rooms, is a somewhat difficult matter, one in which art and utility are apt to come into collision.

Everything in a public library is exposed to a good deal of wear and tear, and consequently paint or varnish within reach of the ground must be avoided.

On the other hand, unless the woodwork is treated in some way it soon shows the dirt to a very objectionable degree; while scouring with soap and water brings out the grain and produces a rough surface. More especially must this be avoided in the case of wooden shelves, where the roughness caused by such scouring is very injurious to the bindings of books.

Probably the most satisfactory method of treating oak is to fume it to a fairly dark tint which will not readily show dirt, and then to wax it.

This treatment, however, disguises merely and does not abolish the evil. The dirt is there, though it is not an eyesore; and many conscientious librarians insist upon highly glazed French-polishing, a treatment which, however, has the disadvantage of showing distinctly the slightest bruise on the surface.

SHELVING AND ACCESSORIES. 31

Even where French-polishing is used, the oak should be previously stained, or treated with a dark "filler."

As to the shelves themselves, various substitutes for wood have been tried. Glass, though difficult to fix, has been used with advantage, and steel shelves * are now made which are very satisfactory.

10. WOODEN BOOKCASES AT SHREWSBURY.

Bookcases.

The bookcases generally used in public libraries are of two forms, single wall-cases and double floor-cases, the former being placed against a wall with shelves facing one way only, the latter standing independently with shelves on either side.

One very essential quality of bookcases is rigidity. Unless, however, the shelves are fixed, this cannot, with an entirely wooden construction, be sufficiently secured except by means of a solid partition (Fig. 10) at the backs of the shelves.

---

* See page 33.

Such a partition has many disadvantages. It adds considerably to the difficulty of thoroughly dusting the shelves: interferes with the circulation of air behind the books (indeed, where floor-cases are used, it materially affects the diffusion of light and air in the room generally); and further makes it easy for books to get hidden accidentally or otherwise at the backs of the shelves.

One fixed shelf about 3 ft. above the floor gives a fair degree of rigidity, but certainly where steps and handles are attached to the cases this is not sufficient.

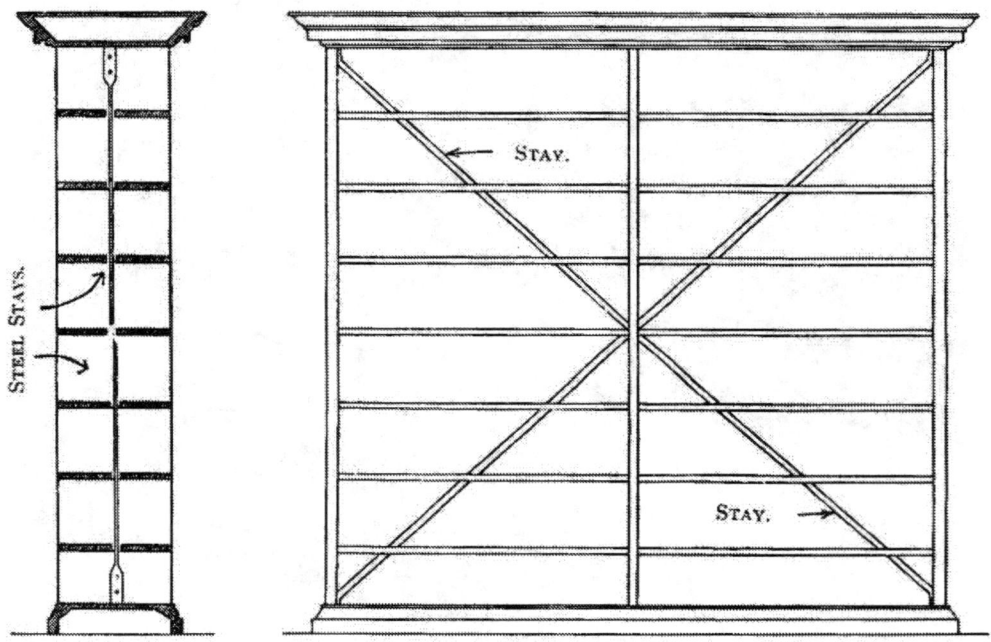

11. Section and Elevation of Wooden Bookcase with Steel Stays in place of Wooden Partition.

The better plan is to use steel stays or braces (Fig. 11).

Where this is done, screens of wire-netting should be fixed at the backs of the shelves to prevent books from being pushed in too far.

A small air space should always be left between a wall-case and the wall.

The uprights of wooden bookcases are generally $1\frac{1}{4}$ in. finished. They should never be placed more than 3 ft. apart, and 2 ft. 9 in. is better. Otherwise the shelves, which are usually $\frac{7}{8}$ in. finished, are apt to sag when filled with books.

Shelves should never be made with square edges in front where

SHELVING AND ACCESSORIES.

these are likely to damage the books. Circular sections, however, cause difficulty when it is desired to affix labels to the fronts of the shelves.

The edges of both shelves and uprights should, however, be slightly rounded (Fig. 12, A).

A very useful section is one which affords fixing for labels between two beads (Fig. 12, B). Steel shelves, also, are made with the upper edge rounded (Fig. 13, A), and a very good form (Fig. 13, B) is sometimes used which, by means of a double bend, gives sufficient rigidity for a 3-ft. bearing with a thickness of ½ in., thus economising ⅜ in. for every tier of shelves.

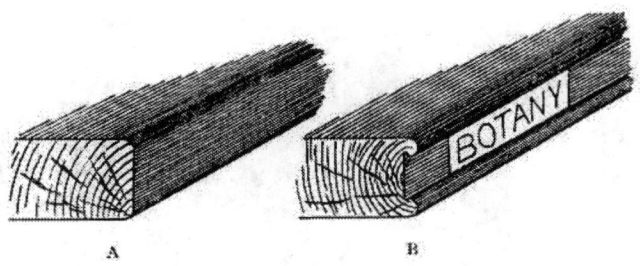

12. SECTIONS OF WOODEN SHELVES.

In some American libraries very excellent open steel shelves are used, but their cost is very considerable.

In order to protect the lowest tier of books in a case from dust and injury generally, a plinth (see Figs. 10 and 11) should be provided to raise them above the floor. This should under no circumstances be less than 2½ in. high; and generally 4 in. should be regarded as the minimum.

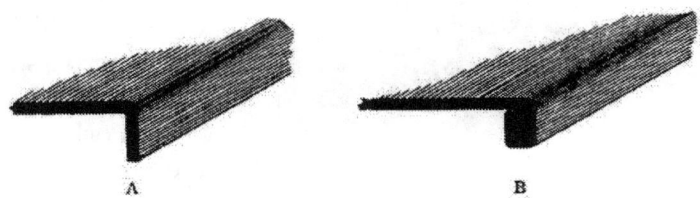

13. SECTIONS OF STEEL SHELVES.

A dust-board at the top of the case is also necessary to protect the books on the top shelf (see Fig. 11). This is sometimes sloped (see Fig. 10) so that the surfaces are visible and accumulated dust cannot escape notice. It is, however, doubtful whether the redistributed dust which is the chief product of the cleaner is not more objectionable than dust resting harmlessly out of sight on the top of the cases.

The height of bookcases is a very important matter. Generally it should not be greater than will allow the books on the top shelf to be reached from the floor; that is to say, the top of the highest shelf should not be greatly in excess of 7 ft. above the floor.*

At the same time, it is important, in order to economise space, to provide as many shelves as possible within such a height.

In a classified library small volumes and large will have to be placed side by side on the same shelf, but quartos and all exceptionally large or oddly shaped volumes are generally located elsewhere, and represented in the classified shelves by wooden dummies bearing the title of the book they represent, and indicating the whereabouts of the volume itself.

14. Bookcases with Projecting Plinth and Handles (Hornsey Public Library).

For the remainder a standard of 10 in. between the shelves has been found the best basis for calculation.

Now 10 in. with $\frac{7}{8}$ in. for each shelf and 4 in. for the plinth gives eight shelves within 7 ft. 6 in., or, more accurately, 7 ft. 6$\frac{1}{8}$ in. from the floor; a height which is within reach of persons of average stature.

Works of fiction average very small, the great majority being no more than 7$\frac{1}{2}$ to 8 in. in height. Consequently, there is seldom any difficulty in accommodating nine fiction shelves within 7 ft. 6 in.

Cornices and dust-boards are, of course, excluded from this calculation.

Although, where the height of the shelving is limited to 7 ft. 6 in., the books on the top shelf are well in view of any but very short-

---

* For height of shelves in children's rooms see Chapter VIII., p. 91.

SHELVING AND ACCESSORIES.

sighted persons, those near the floor are very likely to escape notice; while where the space in front of the shelves is cramped, and stooping consequently difficult, they are as inaccessible as those high up.

Consequently, where the public are not admitted to the shelves, and the shelf-classification does not need the same exactitude, the lowest shelves should be used only for books seldom required.

In open libraries, however, it is on the whole advisable to sacrifice the bottom shelf altogether and provide instead a projecting plinth which will serve as a step (Fig. 14).

The step should not be too high, or a very considerable strain is put upon the bookcases when any one pulls himself up by the handles (see Fig. 19, p. 40) attached to the uprights: indeed high steps are said to be injurious to those who use them, and more especially to women and children. For this reason a step higher than 9 in. is not desirable.

The lowest shelf should, however, be raised sufficiently above the step to protect the books in it from the toes of boots. A height of $1\frac{1}{2}$ to 2 in. is quite sufficient for this purpose, but it is better where the step is not more than 9 in. high to raise the lowest tier of books 3 or 4 in. above the step in order to bring them as much as possible into view.

Where the lowest shelf is raised 3 in. above a 9-in. step the top of the seventh shelf will be 7 ft. $3\frac{1}{4}$ in. above the floor, a height which allows any but very short-sighted persons to scan the highest tier of books with ease; while the 9-in. step brings them within reach of small children.

An improvement on the wooden step is a metal rail supported either by brackets or small stanchions. This form has the advantage of affording less harbourage for dust.

Other forms of steps, together with the handles used in connection with them, will be described later.*

The variation of the depth of books from back to front is not so great as that of their height, while in this dimension an exact correspondence between the size of the book and the depth of the shelf is not so absolutely necessary; that is to say, it is possible, though not desirable, for a volume to project slightly in front of the shelf which supports it.

The great majority of the books in the average lending library are octavos, and therefore the single cases are usually only $7\frac{1}{2}$ in. and the

---

* See pages 40 and 41.

double 15 in. deep, exclusive, of course, of any solid partitions at the backs of the shelves.

A few shelves 9 in. deep should be provided in wall-cases for quartos.

For reference shelves a depth of 9 in. for single and 1 ft. 6 in. for double cases, exclusive as before of partitions, is usually recommended.

Most libraries, however, contain a certain number of folios and other large or odd-shaped books.

These, where they are not accommodated in special cases, will require depths varying from 1 ft. 3 in. to 1 ft. 6 in.

Sometimes deep shelving is provided in the lower part of the ordinary cases, one fixed shelf projecting and forming a ledge where the depth is changed (see Fig. 10).

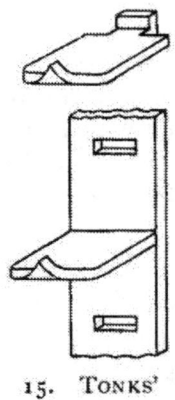

15. TONKS' FITTINGS.

Generally, however, it is better to provide for large volumes one or two special cases of uniform depth, though in closed libraries the ledge is useful as a temporary stand for returned books. If this method is adopted the fixed shelf which forms the ledge should be at a height of 2 ft. 8 in. to 3 ft. above the floor. It should have a nosing in order to give as large a surface as possible on which loose books may be placed.

There remains for consideration one other dimension of books, namely, their thickness. This varies more than either of the others, since it is in no way affected by the different sizes of paper used in the making of books.

It is, however, important that the architect should be able to estimate more or less nearly the number of volumes which a certain amount of shelving may be expected to contain.

Such an estimate can, of course, be only approximate.

In some libraries, for instance, numbers of small pamphlets are reckoned as separate volumes, while in others these are bound together in manilla wrappers or kept in boxes on the shelves.

For library stocks generally nine volumes to 1 ft. linear of shelf is a fair allowance. Taken separately, lending library books may be taken as averaging nine and a half or ten volumes to the foot, and those in a reference library eight and a half to nine: the larger number in each case being that usually adopted in calculating the accommodation.

Though the 10-in. standard for the height of books is a very useful one in working out the height required for the cases, fixed shelves are nowadays very rarely used.

SHELVING AND ACCESSORIES.

It is obvious that in a classified library, where books are grouped by subject and not by size and where old books are being continually replaced by new, fixed shelves would often lead to difficulties. A great many different devices in the form of ratchets and pegs have been used for supporting movable shelves.

The most satisfactory form of fitting for wooden cases is one consisting of metal clips, four to each shelf, which fit into slots in strips

16. STEEL BOOKCASES
(USED AT THE PATENT OFFICE LIBRARY, LONDON, KINGSTON PUBLIC LIBRARY, AND ELSEWHERE).

of metal let into the wooden uprights (Fig. 15. See also Fig. 10). These clips fit closely under the shelf so that they do not damage the books beneath. The slots are spaced at intervals of 1 in. Great care must be taken that the grooves behind the strips are properly cut to the required widths and depths, and that the strips are accurately fitted with the slots level.

A form of steel bookcase (Fig. 16) is made which gives an adjustment to the smallest fraction of an inch, and which is generally very satisfactory, although architects are often discontented with its æsthetic qualities.

With these cases the shelves can be moved up or down when full of books, a great advantage over the other system, in which the shelves must be emptied and the clips taken out and replaced one by one.

Where movable shelves are used it is a great convenience if they are interchangeable. Consequently, it is best that all the shelves in a library should be of a uniform length, which, as has been said, should not be more than 2 ft. 9 in. or at most 3 ft.

Doors are not generally used on the bookcases in public libraries. Where, however, they are necessary, open wire panels are preferable to glass, as they do not interfere with the ventilation of the cases.

Dwarf Cases.—Low bookcases, known as dwarf cases, are often used where those of the full height would interfere with the lighting of the room, or are for any other reason impracticable (see Fig. 66).

They are often used in reading rooms for directories and other quick-reference books, the top providing a convenient support for a book while it is being consulted.

In reading rooms dwarf cases placed away from the walls have the advantage that they do not interfere with ventilation or supervision to the same extent as high cases.

Storage Cases. — Where books not much in use are stored separately from the main stock, the cases which contain them do not necessarily differ from those described above; though when they are right away from the public view they are often made in a very plain and cheap form. Since too quick access is not in this case of great importance they are often of a considerably greater height than that recommended for library shelving generally, the upper shelves being reached usually by means of ladders.

A useful form of portable deal shelving is made which can be fitted up in lengths of 3 ft., and can be extended from time to time as required.

A good and cheap form of iron bookcase for storage purposes is the old American system of gas-pipe stacking which may with advantage be used also for unbound newspapers, map and print cases, and the like.

Sometimes, however, the available storage space becomes filled up, and some method of further increasing its capacity is found necessary.

This may be attained by the use of an ingenious device by which

SHELVING AND ACCESSORIES.

bookcases are hung on rollers which run on overhead girders (Fig. 17). The cases can then be packed closely together, and when a volume is required the case containing it is pulled out into a gangway and pushed back again after the book has been taken out.*

Show Cases.—In many libraries special cases are provided for the display of new volumes or works on special or topical subjects. These are, of course, far more useful if open, so that readers may glance through the pages; for the cover and title cannot be considered reliable indications of what the volume contains. Even if the cases are closed it is best that the books should have some of their title-pages rather than their backs displayed.

Closed show cases are made with either wire or glass fronts, and are, when fitted on a counter, open at the back. Wire is preferable to glass as giving better ventilation.

Revolving Cases.—Revolving bookcases are extremely useful in a librarian's room, and may often be used with advantage in public rooms. In the former case a height of about 2 ft. 8 in. is to be preferred, as the top may then be used as a table while the librarian is sitting at his desk.

In public rooms revolving cases are sometimes used for encyclopædias or directories, and a table-top at a height of from 3 ft. to 3 ft. 6 in. is useful for the consultation of quick-reference volumes.

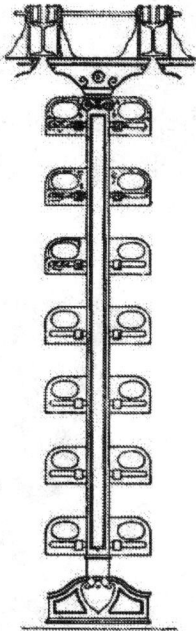

17. ROLLING BOOK-CASES (USED AT THE INDIA OFFICE LIBRARY, LONDON, AND ELSEWHERE).

Folio Cases.—As has been already stated, large folios are usually provided with special accommodation. It is generally considered that they are best kept flat on their sides instead of upright, since the latter position, unless they are properly supported, allows the large pages to sag and strain the binding.

A double case (Fig. 18) with reading slopes above is very useful. The shelves should each have a brass handle on the front edge, and should be so made that they can be pulled out; for if the volumes

---

* See also Chapter VI., pp. 67 and 68.

themselves have to be dragged out, their bindings are likely to get damaged. In the case of very heavy books it is advisable to have the

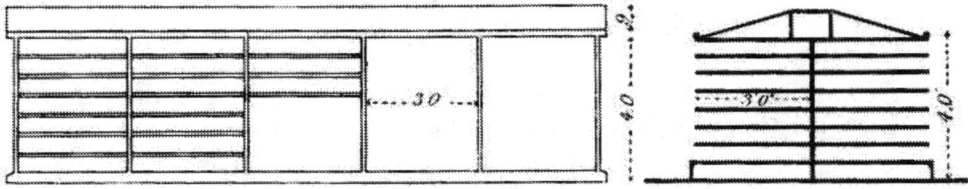

18. FOLIO CASE FOR USE IN PUBLIC LIBRARIES.

shelves on rollers instead of ordinary supports, in order that they may be more easily pulled out.

The tops are sometimes used as show cases.

There are many other methods of accommodating folios which need not, however, be dealt with in the present work.

Steps, Ladders, and Galleries.—Since it is usually necessary to economise floor space, it is seldom advisable that the height of the shelves should be less than that indicated (page 34), while sometimes it is necessary that it should be more. If so, some form of step should be provided by which persons of short stature may raise themselves when it is necessary to handle volumes on the top shelf.

Two kinds of continuous step have been already mentioned above.

Handles must, of course, be provided in connection with the steps, and it is important that there should be one handle on each, and not, as is often the case, one on every other upright.

With wooden shelving, when the plinth is a low one, detached steps are fastened to the uprights at a height of from 9 to 12 in. above the floor.

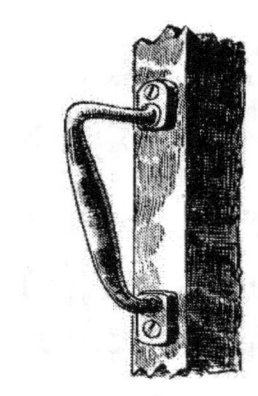

19. SWINGING STEP AND IMPROVED GRIP AS USED AT HULL, KILMARNOCK, &c.

A useful step is one which, though always ready for use, is brushed aside if any one touches it when passing, and then returns to its position (Fig. 19). This form possesses the further advantage that it does not

SHELVING AND ACCESSORIES.

entail any cutting away of the woodwork, and presents no rough edges or screw-heads where these might damage the books. The handles provided with it are also very convenient in shape.

Occasionally it is necessary owing to lack of space, and more particularly in store-rooms used for books seldom wanted and where quick access to the volumes is of no great importance, to provide cases of such a height that steps and handles are an insufficient assistance for reaching the books at the top, and ladders of some sort have to be provided. Even with cases of moderate height, ladders are often a great help in scrutinising the upper shelves, and in dusting and arranging the books.

Step ladders are, of course, to be preferred to those with rungs, and a form very commonly used in libraries is illustrated (Fig. 20).

They should be light and easily moved.

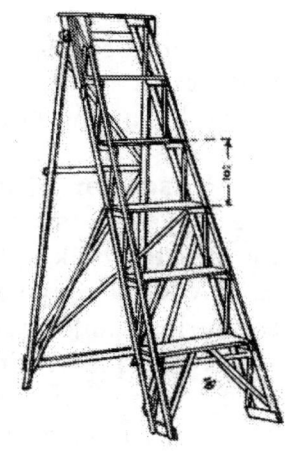

20. STEP LADDER.

There are various devices used to prevent ladders placed against the face of the shelves from damaging the books, while sometimes the top of the ladder is hooked on to a fixed brass rail in front of the shelving, along which it can be moved in either direction (see Fig. 67, p. 95).

Where the floor space is insufficient to accommodate all the books within reach from the floor, the use of galleries is far preferable to that of ladders. Even this, however, must be regarded merely as the lesser of two evils. It is, of course, necessary that the room should be of a sufficient height to allow head room above and below, but 14 ft., or even slightly less, will suffice.

The form which a gallery will take depends, of course, on the arrangement of the bookcases.

Galleries should, as a rule, be such as to obstruct as little as possible the free diffusion of light and air. They are usually constructed of iron, though sometimes with wooden floors. More often, however, they have either roughened plate-glass panels or a grille.

A hand-rail should, of course, be provided, and this may with advantage be fitted with small desks for the inspection or consultation of books. There should also be either a rail within a few inches of the gallery floor level, or a fillet of some sort at the outer edge to prevent slipping; while the space between this and the hand-rail should be sufficiently protected by horizontal rails which intercept less light than vertical balusters.

Galleries should never be less than 2 ft. 4 in. wide.

Chapter V.

FITTINGS, FURNITURE, AND APPLIANCES.

Materials.—The greater part of the fittings and furniture of public libraries are made of wood, the particular wood differing according to the requirements of the various fittings and their various parts. As with bookcases, so with other fittings, oak is very largely used. With regard to the finish of woodwork for fittings in general the same considerations apply as in the case of shelving, which has been dealt with at the beginning of the preceding chapter.

Cases for Maps and Prints.—In public libraries of an average size very little special accommodation for maps or prints is required, the greater bulk, when not framed and displayed on the walls, being usually kept in boxes on the shelves or storage racks, while there is a growing tendency in favour of maps in atlas form.

Consequently, for the generality of such libraries, a simple and cheap form of case with sliding drawers is sufficient, which may with advantage have a sloping top, on which the maps may be placed for consultation.*

Where maps and prints are kept unbound in large drawers, there is often a good deal of difficulty in making the drawers sufficiently rigid without at the same time making them too heavy. Various devices have been tried to attain this end, but the most satisfactory method is to make the bottoms of corrugated iron, lined, of course, with leather or some other soft material which will not harbour moth.

Many means have been tried for excluding dust from the drawers. Indiarubber tubing has the advantage that it is not liable to the attacks of moth, though it is rather expensive owing to the need of frequent renewal.

Sometimes the front and part of the bottom of the drawer is

---

* See description and illustration of folio cases, Chapter IV., pp. 39 and 40, the requirements of which are similar.

FITTINGS, FURNITURE, AND APPLIANCES.

hinged and fitted with springs, in order that large sheets may be more easily taken out; while a small jointed lid at the back of the drawer prevents the ends of loose sheets from turning up and getting damaged.

The plan of accommodating wall-maps on spring-rollers is not generally recommended for public libraries, except possibly in the case of a few local maps. Revolving screens are very useful for the display of prints, photographs, and manuscripts.

Exhibition Cases.—Sometimes glass cases for the display of manuscripts or rare books are provided on the tops of folio cases or map-cases. For other collections various sorts of glazed exhibition or museum cases are employed.

Storage Cases for Files of Periodicals.*—Generally any form of accommodation is good enough for storage of newspapers and magazines. They are usually filed in boxes, or in cheap wooden shelving. In large libraries, however, special provision should be made; iron or steel racks with corrugated iron shelves being recommended.

21. STANDARD RACK FOR MAGAZINES (BERMONDSEY AND LEWISHAM PUBLIC LIBRARIES).

Racks for Current Magazines and Periodicals.—Though there are many different methods of accommodating in the reading rooms the current numbers of magazines, technical journals, and other periodicals, it is not proposed under the present head to discuss the comparative merits or demerits of this system or that, but only to describe one or two of the special fittings.

Racks for current periodicals are made to stand either on tables or on the floor, or to hang on the walls.

Various forms of table-rack may be seen in almost every public library, and need not be described here.

---

* Racks and stands for files of newspapers in reading rooms are separately dealt with below (page 50).

Reading tables with sloping tops are sometimes made with a well to hold magazines, but this system is not generally recommended.

There are various forms of wall racks in use. On the whole, those showing the lower part of the periodical (Fig. 21) are preferable, since with these the titles printed on the special covers can all be brought to the same level, whatever the size of the publication. With this fitting, however, it is important that all the periodicals should be kept in covers with the titles printed on them near the lower edge.

A small wall-rack for time-tables is also very useful (Fig. 22).

22. RACK FOR TIME-TABLES.

Directory-Stands.—Directory-stands with either a table or desk in front are very useful.

Peerages, year-books, and so on may also be shelved in this manner.

There are innumerable forms of directory-stand made, and examples may be seen in every public library.

Reading Tables, Desks, and Easels.—Tables for the reading rooms of public libraries should be solidly made, of oak for preference, though some authorities recommend walnut or mahogany. The tops are sometimes made of teak, and in some cases plate glass has been used (Fig. 23).

Longitudinal rails near the floor are best omitted (Fig. 24), as they are used as scrapers by those sitting at the tables. If they are adopted, however, they should be protected by rubber (Fig. 25), or, better still, some substance which needs less frequent renewal. The best height for reading tables is 30 in. (less of course for children*), and the breadth, where both sides are used for readers, should never be less than 3 ft. Indeed 3 ft. 6 in. should usually be allowed, or, where there is sufficient space, 4 ft. As a general rule a minimum length of 2 ft. to 2 ft. 3 in. should be allowed for each reader, and 2 ft. 6 in. is better; while for especially studious work a still more liberal spacing is desir-

---

* Chapter VIII., p. 90.

FITTINGS, FURNITURE, AND APPLIANCES.

able. In the case of magazine readers, however, 20 in. is often considered sufficient.

Tables of great length, that is to say of more than 9 or 10 ft., should be avoided in public libraries.

Reading tables can be made either with flat (Fig. 26, A) or with sloping tops (Fig. 26, B). The latter should be very slightly sloped, and

23. READING TABLES WITH PLATE-GLASS TOPS
(MASSACHUSETTS STATE LIBRARY).

should have a fillet at the bottom of the slope, otherwise great inconvenience is caused by books, papers, and pencils slipping and rolling down.

Small stands for umbrellas are often fixed to the ends of reading tables, so that readers may keep them in sight.

In rooms used for magazine reading only, the size of the tables is not so important as is the provision of free space round them. Small

24. Reading Tables (Eastbourne Public Library).

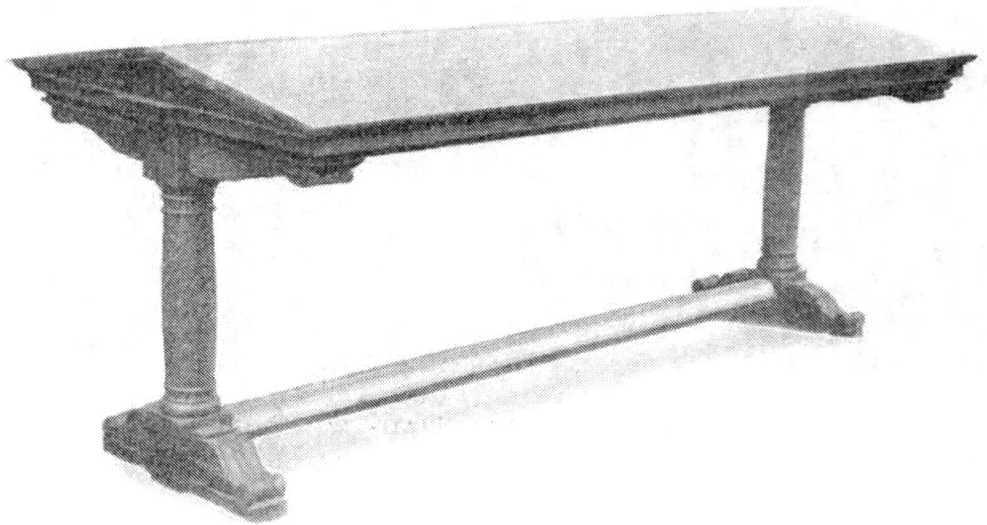

25. Reading Tables (Hammersmith Public Library).

H. T. Hare, f.r.i.b.a., *Architect.*

tables, not too close together, are most suitable. Magazine readers should be able to push their chairs back and rest the magazines on their knees.

FITTINGS, FURNITURE, AND APPLIANCES.

Thus a table 5 ft. by 2 ft. 10 in. will accommodate one magazine reader at each end and three at each side, while similarly a table 6 ft. by 3 ft. is sufficient for eight persons, and a table 3 ft. square for four.

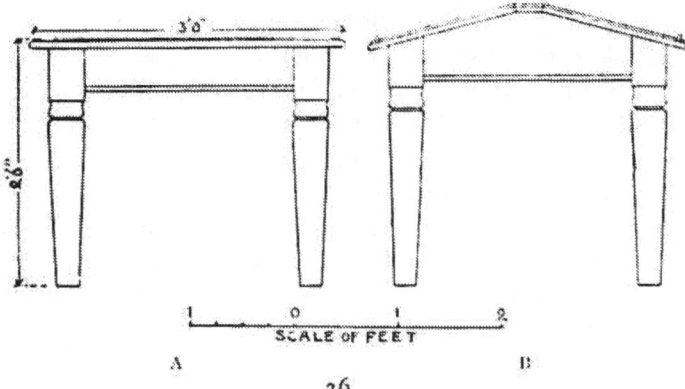

26.

Circular or oval tables are sometimes used in magazine rooms and relieve the appearance of the room to some extent of monotony and formality. In American libraries circular tables are a great deal used.

27. READING TABLES WITH SCREENS.
(CORNELL UNIVERSITY LIBRARY, ITHACA, N.Y.).

For especially studious work not only liberal table space but as complete isolation as possible is required.

In the British Museum reading room 4 ft. 2 in. run of table is allowed to each reader, a screen shields him from his opposite neighbour, and many conveniences in the way of easels, pen-racks, and other accessories are provided.

Public libraries cannot afford either such elaborate fittings or so much space; though a form of table adopted in an American University library may be recommended (Fig. 27).

The privacy of a reference reader may, however, be to a large extent secured by the provision of tables 2 ft. broad, which accommodate readers on one side only. These are usually made with sloping tops, and allow from 2 ft. 6 in. to 3 ft. for each reader.

28. SINGLE TABLE FOR REFERENCE READERS (LIVERPOOL PUBLIC LIBRARY, &c.).

Detached tables (Fig. 28) for reference rooms have also been recommended. These may have a screen added in front with accommodation for pens, paper, and books, and also an extension flap (see Fig. 66).*

In small towns, however, the reference room of the average public library is not much frequented, and often a reader can get the whole side of a long table to himself, in which case he is better off in respect of table space and privacy than if he had a table such as that illustrated.

Various kinds of reading easels are used in public libraries. These may either be made as part of a table (in which they lie flush with the surface when not in use), or they may be entirely detached.

Newspaper Reading-Slopes.—Until daily papers can be produced in some more compact form, or until their admission in public libraries is much restricted, their accommodation will of necessity

---

* See J. D. Brown's "Manual of Library Economy," § 220, Fig. 75.

FITTINGS, FURNITURE, AND APPLIANCES.

involve a somewhat excessive sacrifice of space. Though back numbers can be stored more or less closely, every current issue in a reading room requires a sufficient space to allow of its being opened. For this purpose the papers are fastened to reading slopes before which, in most cases, the readers stand.

These fittings are made either as single wall slopes (see Figs. 30 and 62) or as double stands (Figs. 29 and 61).

Since not only the size of newspapers but the stature of readers is

29. DOUBLE NEWSPAPER SLOPE (HAMMERSMITH PUBLIC LIBRARY).
H. T. Hare, F.R.I.B.A., *Architect*.

liable to variation, the dimensions of these slopes must be carefully considered. While a very steep slope causes the pages to sag, if it is not steep enough it is difficult for a short person to read the letterpress at the top of the paper.

The dimensions shown (Fig. 30) are those which have been found in practice to produce the most satisfactory results.

A projecting metal rail, upon which the readers may rest their arms, should always be fixed at the bottom of the slope: otherwise they are sure to lean on the slope itself and tear the papers.

At the top there is usually a board about 6 in. high, on which are fixed tablets with the titles of the papers boldly printed.

With regard to length, 4 ft. run of slope is usually allowed for each paper, but 3 ft. 6 in., more especially in the case of continuous wall slopes, would be generally sufficient.

Wall slopes, when possible, should be used in preference to the double stands. Their advantages are many: the positions of the various papers are more readily seen, supervision is more complete, there is less interference with the diffusion of air, and considerably less waste of space.

Recently several libraries have been fitted with slopes for seated readers (Fig. 31), on which the weekly illustrated papers are usually displayed.

For fastening papers to reading slopes there are a number of different appliances in existence.

Very useful fasteners consist of a pair of screw clips which can be adjusted to papers of different heights, or rods which press the centre fold of the paper against the slope. For illustrated papers revolving holders save a great deal of inconvenience. All of these can be seen in any public library.

Sometimes a few back numbers of papers are kept in the reading rooms. In this case newspaper file-stands or racks (Figs. 32 and 33) are useful.

In cases where back numbers of weekly and other periodicals are kept in reading rooms for reference, along with the current numbers, the boxes and special stands used in the Patent Office Library, London, are strongly recommended.

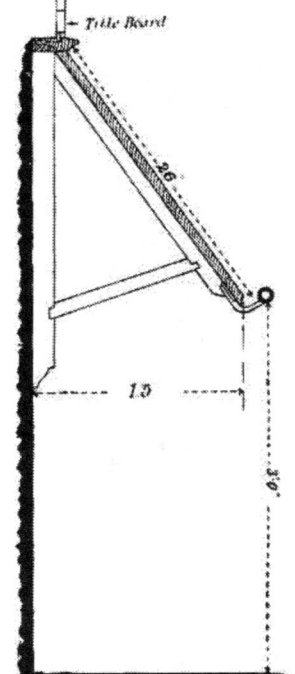

30. SECTION OF NEWSPAPER WALL SLOPE (KINGSTON PUBLIC LIBRARY).

Reading Room Chairs.—For public reading rooms the chairs must be strongly made, and arm-chairs are preferred, as these secure sufficient elbow-room. Wooden saddle-seats are, of course, to be in every way preferred to cane or upholstery. Fixed revolving seats where the space is cramped, have sometimes to be used, but they are very undesirable, as if their position suits one reader it does not suit another, while there is always the danger of the floor being damaged. A better plan is to fasten the chair by a cord to a staple in the floor.

FITTINGS, FURNITURE, AND APPLIANCES.

Where the floor is of wood the legs of chairs should be shod with indiarubber pads.

Where cork carpet is used the legs should have broad feet that will not cut the carpet when the chair is tilted, or better still a flush rail joining the feet behind and on each side, the edges and corners being of course rounded.

The height of the seat should be $16\frac{1}{2}$ or 17 in., except, of course, in juvenile reading rooms.*

Various accessories to library chairs, such as folding trays, hat rails, umbrella clips and so on, have been suggested.†

31. SLOPE FOR SEATED READERS (EASTBOURNE PUBLIC LIBRARY).

P. S. Robson, Architect.

Catalogue Fittings.†—There are five distinct methods of displaying catalogues, whether printed or written. These have been named: page, card, sheaf, placard, and panoramic.‡ The last-named need not be dealt with here.

The old-fashioned page catalogue is seldom used in public libraries nowadays, owing to the difficulty of making additions and at the same time preserving the alphabetical order.

---

* See Chapter VIII., p. 90.
† See J. D. Brown's "Manual of Library Economy," § 230.
‡ *Library*, 1894, pp. 45-66, article on "Mechanical Methods of Displaying Catalogues and Indexes," by J. D. Brown. A very full account of the various methods will be found in his "Library Economy," chapter xxiii. The present work merely deals with the fittings which affect architectural considerations.

In order to overcome the disadvantages of this form, the card catalogue has come into use.

The most usual form of card catalogue is a cabinet with drawers which may stand on a counter or on a special table (Fig. 34).

The disadvantage of this form is that one person may monopolise a very large number of entries, since, while a drawer remains partially in the cabinet, not only the cards it contains itself but those in the drawer below, and even in that above, are inaccessible. Consequently it is best that single drawers should be used, that is, drawers containing one row each of cards; and that each drawer should be made so that it may be removed and con-

32. STANDARD RACK FOR CURRENT FILES OF NEWSPAPERS (SHEFFIELD PUBLIC LIBRARY).

sulted away from the cabinet. For this purpose a table and chairs should be provided near the cabinet, but not immediately under it.

The construction of the drawers or trays will be sufficiently explained by the accompanying illustration (Fig. 35).

Each drawer is usually 15 in. long, and will contain about 1,000 cards, together with the necessary guide cards.

33. WALL RACK FOR CURRENT FILES OF NEWSPAPERS (KINGSTON PUBLIC LIBRARY).

Sheaf catalogues (Fig. 36) have the advantage over card catalogues that they are divided into smaller sections, and consequently each consultant monopolises fewer entries.

FITTINGS, FURNITURE, AND APPLIANCES.

Such catalogues may be kept either on racks or in ordinary pigeon-holes.

Placard catalogues are largely used for displaying the names of new books. A useful form of adjustable placard* with xylonite slips and movable entries is sometimes used.

Similar frames are used in reading rooms for displaying the names of periodicals.

Charging Appliances.

Ledger Charging.—Besides the ledger itself, which hardly concerns the architect, and the counter, which will be described below,† ledger charging requires no special furniture; though sometimes, where this system is used, the counter is made with a sloping top, or a movable desk is placed on it. Whichever

34. CARD-CATALOGUE CABINET WITH SLIDING SHELVES.

35. DRAWER OF CARD-CATALOGUE CABINET.

method is used, the top of the slope should be 3 ft. 6 in. above

---

* See J. D. Brown's "Manual of Library Economy," § 364.
† See pages 57, 58, and 76.

the floor. The system is, however, so little used in public libraries to-day that it is unnecessary to consider it further in the present work.

Indicators.—The indicator is a device by which both readers and staff can see whether any particular book is in or out; and there are many forms of indicator which at the same time record the date of issue and the name of the borrower. They are usually rather unsightly machines, but their appearance can often be improved by being set

36. Sheaf Catalogue as used at Islington Public Library.

in frames or screens (see Fig. 51, p. 72).

The number of indicators that have been invented is considerable, but it will be sufficient in the present instance to describe one or two forms only.

The indicator most commonly used is the Cotgreave (Fig. 37). "It consists of a wooden or iron frame, fitted with minute zinc shelves, generally one hundred in a column. Upon each of these shelves is placed a small metal-bound ledger (3 in. by 1 in.), containing a number of leaves, ruled and beaded for the number of borrower's ticket, and date of issue; also date of return or other items as may be required, numbered or lettered at each end, and arranged numerically in the frames. One part of it is also lettered for entries of date of purchase, title of book, &c. The metal case has turned-up ends, and the numbers

37. Cotgreave Indicator.

appear on a ground coloured red at one end, and blue at the other, one colour showing books *out*, the other, books *in*; other colours may be used if preferred. The *out* numbers can be covered altogether with a date slide if required. The change of colour is effected by simply

FITTINGS, FURNITURE, AND APPLIANCES.

reversing the ledger in the indicator frame. The public side of the indicator is protected by glass.

"The *modus operandi* is as follows:—A borrower having chosen a book from the catalogue, consults the indicator, and finding the required number to be on *blue*, denoting *in*, asks for the book corresponding, at the same time tendering his library ticket. The assistant withdraws the indicator ledger, makes the necessary entries, inserts borrower's ticket, and reverses the ledger, which then shows the *red* colour, signifying *out*. He then hands out the book asked for. The borrower's ticket will remain in this number until he changes his book, when his ticket will, of course, be transferred to the next number required, and the returned number will be reversed again, showing by the blue colour that the book it represents is again *in*, and is immediately available to any other reader requiring it. The entries need not be made at the time of issue, but may stand over until a more convenient time.

"When a book is not required the ticket is returned to the borrower, and acts as a receipt, exonerating him from liabilities."

In a still earlier type* the tickets themselves could be seen from either side and indicated either that the book was in or out.

The only other form that need be mentioned is the Chivers' Indicator, of which the following description may be quoted:—

"This consists of a series of wooden blocks, each of which is numbered with 250 numbers in gilt figures, and each number has a slot under it large enough to hold book-card with red coloured or white ends, bearing the same number as the slot. These blocks can be built into columns of 1,000 with the numbers running consecutively, the whole being lodged in a glazed frame (Fig. 38). This indicator differs from other varieties in having the numbers qualified by the red or white line of the card under the numbers to indicate books *in;* when the slot is blank the book is *out*. The withdrawal of the book-card is the method of indicating books out, and it is the union

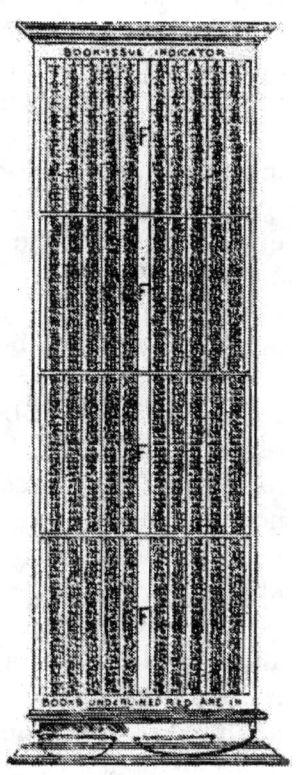

38.
CHIVERS' INDICATOR.

---

* The Elliot.

of this card with the borrower's card which forms the basis of the subsequent registration. When a book is issued the assistant withdraws the card from the recorder and places it in the reader's ticket, which is formed like a pocket, fetches the book, stamps it with the date of issue, and so completes the transaction at the moment of service. Afterwards the readers' pocket tickets containing the book-cards are assembled and arranged according to classes in numerical order. They are then posted by book and reader numbers only on to a daily issue sheet or register, and the date of issue is stamped on each book-card, if this has not already been done at the moment of service. The conjoined book-and-reader cards are then placed in a tray bearing the date of issue, in the order of classes and book numbers as may be needful."

For architects the most important consideration connected with indicators is their size in relation to the number of volumes registered.

In the case of the two indicators described it will be seen from the illustrations that the Cotgreave requires a length of 5 ft. 2 in. for every 4,000, that is, 15 in. for every 1,000 volumes, and the Chivers, $11\frac{1}{2}$ in. for every 1,000,* while in this indicator the height of the highest row of figures is considerably less.

In planning a lending library with indicators the form to be employed should be ascertained, and the requisite space for the registration of the books calculated. Moreover, if a high indicator is to be used, care must be taken that the counter on which it stands is not higher than 2 ft. 6 in.

Indicators may also be used for periodicals either in lending libraries or reading rooms.

When this method of issue is used in reading rooms for magazines and periodicals, a more simple form is used. This may consist of a frame with columns containing narrow blocks of wood with the titles mounted on them and holes drilled opposite each, into which may be fitted a wooden peg, black at one end and white at the other: the one denoting the absence, the other the presence of a periodical.

Card-Charging Appliances.—Though it is not proposed to describe in detail the various methods of recording the issue and return of books by means of cards, a general idea of the system most usually adopted may be given.

---

* The length required per 1,000 volumes by other indicators is as follows:—The Duplex, 32 in.: the Elliot, 36 in. (or 24 in. for 1,250 in a more compact form): the Bonner, 20 in.: the Morgan, 15 in.; and the Simplex, 11 in.

FITTINGS, FURNITURE, AND APPLIANCES.

Each book in the library is represented by a card, usually 4 in. by 2½ in., ruled with columns for recording date of issue and return. These cards bear the same numbers as the books, and are arranged in numerical order in trays fitted with rods and adjustable angle blocks (Fig. 39). This set of trays is kept at one side of the issue desk, and at the other another set of issue trays is provided, furnished with date and fine guides.

When a book is issued the book-card representing it is withdrawn from the card tray, the date recorded, and the card then placed in a manilla pocket together with the reader's card (Fig. 40). These conjoined cards are arranged numerically behind the date-guide of the day in the issue trays mentioned above.

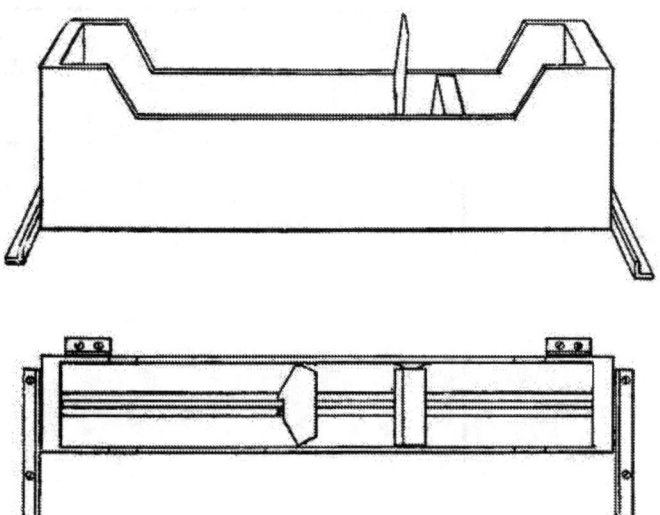

39. CARD-CHARGING TRAY.

Each issue tray will hold approximately 350 conjoined cards, and the number of trays required depends on the average daily issue. As the books are returned their respective cards are withdrawn from the issue trays and replaced in the book-card trays. The system shows overdues automatically.

There are various accessories, such as small brass angles for holding sets of trays together on the counter. A sorting tray for holding the conjoined cards at the counter before filing in the issue trays is generally provided.

Trays for borrowers' vouchers are generally fitted to the counter.

Sometimes the book-cards are kept in pockets in the books themselves and the method of issue is thus considerably quicker.

Counters.—Counters are used in public libraries chiefly for the issue and receipt of books, but their requirements vary according to the method of their use.

The public side of a counter is subject to a good deal of

wear and tear. In order to protect them from kicks they are usually undercut.

The appearance of such a counter being, however, rather unsightly and reminiscent of a public-house bar, a vertical section with glazed brick nogging* is sometimes substituted.

The height should be 3 ft. except where indicators have to be accommodated, when 2 ft. 6 in. is preferable. The top, which is often of teak, should generally be 2 ft. wide.

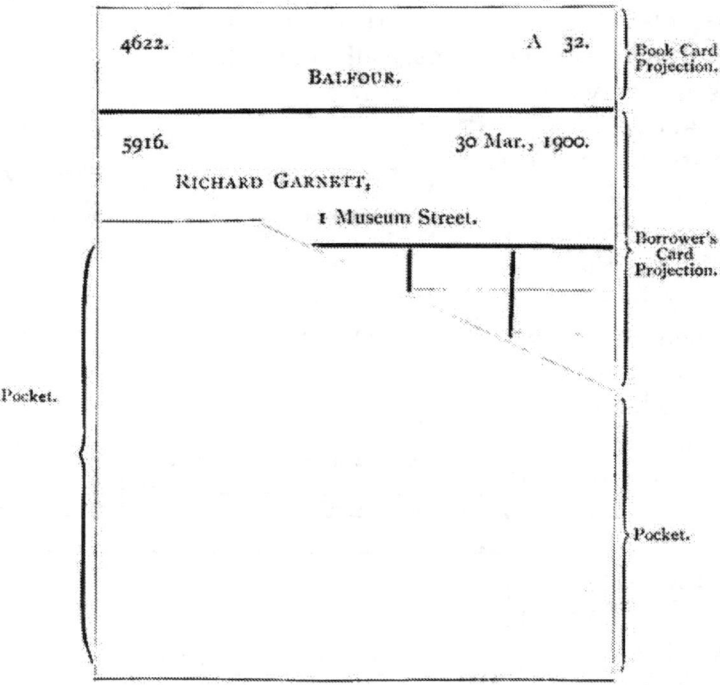

40. COMBINED BOOK AND BORROWER'S CARDS IN POCKET.

It is an advantage to fit up the inside with shelves, cupboards, and drawers; and a counter with a well for trays, which can be covered with a roll-top and locked, is very useful. These and other details vary according to the particular purposes for which the counter is to be used, and will be further described in connection with lending libraries (see pp. 72, 73, Fig. 52).

Wickets.—Wickets are usually required for open-access lending libraries, and sometimes in other places. The height should not be

---

* See Fig. 51, p. 72.

FITTINGS, FURNITURE, AND APPLIANCES.

less than 4 ft., as in some libraries dogs have been found to stray in and jump low wickets. They should be made of oak and should not be fitted with handles, since they can be opened by the top rail when the latch is freed, and will shut automatically. Treadle latches (Fig. 41) are used with open-access wickets.

Partitions, Screens, and Barriers.—There is a decided tendency in public libraries to omit as far as possible solid internal walls. Their place is taken to a great extent by glazed partitions or screens, which facilitate supervision and assist the diffusion of light.

The choice between high partitions and low screens 7 to 8 ft. high must depend largely on the particular circumstances.

Generally speaking, the former are more useful for preventing sounds in one room from permeating to another; but, when quiet is preserved, as it should be throughout, this advantage is to some extent nullified. In the case, however, of rooms intended for special study or research, high partitions should always be preferred.

Low screens, on the other hand, allow a more

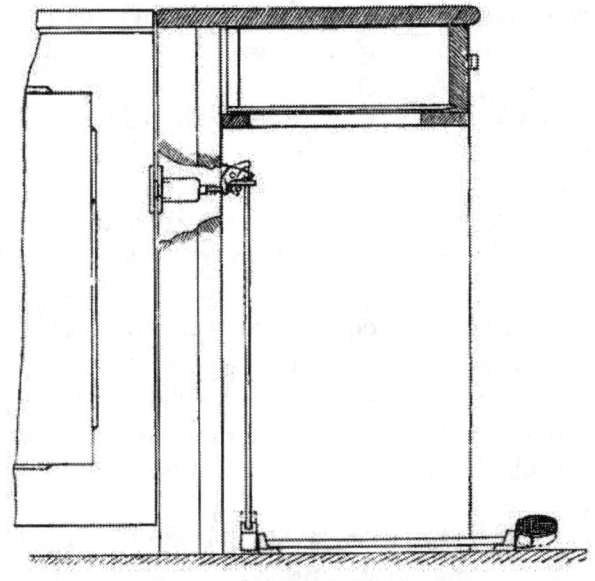

41. TREADLE LATCH.

free diffusion of light and air, and involve less cleaning; though here again, in large libraries where one or more rooms are sometimes closed, openings above the screens may lead to wastefulness in heating.

Glazed partitions or screens should be constructed in oak for preference, and unless the dimensions are affected by fittings, should generally be glazed from a height of from 4 ft. to 4 ft. 6 in. above the floor, more especially where a less height would enable readers sitting in one room to overlook those in another. Wooden sash-bars, with movable fillets, screws, and cups, are on the whole to be preferred to lead lights, as they are less easily damaged. The panes should not be too small.

The aprons should be panelled and finished with a strong plain skirting.

An example of a glazed screen is shown below (see Fig. 66).

Various forms of barriers are employed to divide rooms or to keep readers away from book-shelves. A rope supported by metal uprights is the cheapest, though some form of metal grille with an oak or walnut hand-rail is often used.

A height of 2 ft. 8 in. is sufficient unless the barrier is perforce close to the shelves which it is meant to protect. In this case it should be of such height as to prevent a tall man from leaning over and reaching the books.

Care must be taken where wood block floors are used that a proper fixing is provided for barriers.*

Miscellaneous Fittings and Furniture.—A great proportion of the fittings and furniture required in a library building are in no way special to library work, and will consequently only be mentioned in describing the requirements of various rooms and departments. There are, however, one or two which may be specially insisted upon.

The provision of umbrella stands and clips in connection with tables and chairs in reading rooms has already been mentioned. Another plan is to place small portable umbrella stands in various parts of the reading rooms.

Waste-paper boxes or baskets should also be provided in reference rooms especially, and fire-resisting bins for accumulations of waste paper are required in large libraries.

Good English clocks with legible dials should be placed in conspicuous positions in the public rooms. They should not tick loudly or strike, and should be so placed as to be easily accessible for regulation. In large libraries it often means a very great saving of time and trouble if an electric synchronising clock is placed in one room and simple dials connected to it in others.

---

* See Chapter II., p. 6.

Chapter VI.

BOOK ROOMS.

In the present chapter it is not proposed to deal with those rooms which combine the function of a reading room with that of a book store, but with those intended exclusively for the accommodation of books.

In such rooms it is obvious that, in order to avoid waste, as much as possible of the floor space must be utilised.

In ordinary rectangular rooms this end is usually attained by placing double floor-cases at right angles to two of the walls; the remaining two, and sometimes all four, being fitted with wall-cases (Fig. 42).

With such a system, the closer the spacing of the cases, the greater will be the storage capacity of any given area. This spacing will depend upon the width of the gangways between the faces of the shelves, and these gangways must,

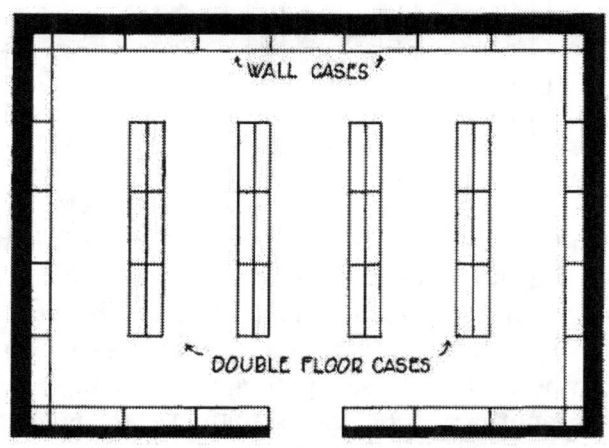

42. Book Room fitted with Wall and Floor Cases.

of course, be adequate for the traffic which will be necessary, while the amount of traffic will vary considerably in different circumstances, according, for instance, as the shelves are open to the public or to the staff only, and according as the books they accommodate are much or little in demand.

In book rooms which are accessible to the staff only gangways 2 ft. 6 in. wide are sometimes considered sufficient, but 3 ft. should rather be the minimum. Indeed, where a number of books in very frequent use are shelved together, 3 ft. 6 in., or, better still, 3 ft. 9 in., should be allowed.

Where the public are admitted to the shelves, the gangways should be as a rule not less than 4 ft. or 4 ft. 6 in. wide, and a width of 5 ft. is desirable where space allows. At the same time, by a judicious disposition of the books upon the shelves, gangways as narrow as 3 ft. 6 in. may sometimes be made to serve their purpose without causing congestion.

In all book rooms, but more especially in those accessible to the public, a space should be left between the ends of the floor-cases and the walls to which they are set at right angles. Otherwise a good deal of congestion and inconvenience is likely to ensue, especially if the gangways are long and narrow. A space of 3 ft., or even 2 ft. 6 in., will often suffice where an outlet merely is required or where the room is used by the staff only, in which case spaces at the

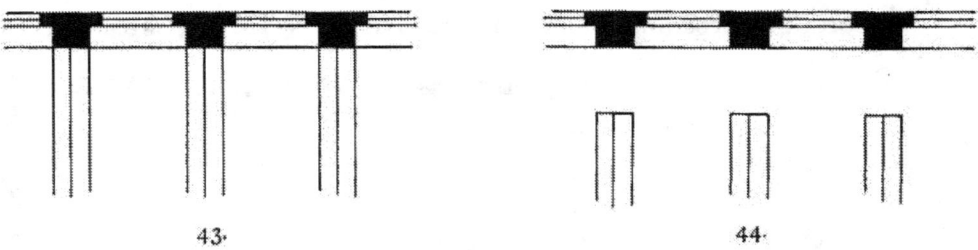

43.   44.

end of every other case are often sufficient (*cf.* Fig. 46). Otherwise, if the end walls are shelved, 4 ft. or 4 ft. 6 in. should be left.

In no case, however, whether the shelves are open to the public or to the staff only, should the cases be of a greater length than 15 ft. without transverse openings. In fact, where the public are admitted a length of not more than 12 ft. is desirable. The width of the transverse gangways must, of course, vary according to the amount of traffic with which they have to cope. For the public they should usually be not less than 3 ft., for the staff 2 ft. 6 in. will suffice, though, where such gangways take the main traffic of the room, greater widths are of course necessary.

With regard to lighting, as has been said above, vertical lights are for many reasons preferable in book rooms to top-lights, and, where such can be utilised, it is of course most important that the windows should be so disposed that not only is no light intercepted by the ends of the cases, but that the faces of the shelves are well illumined, so that

BOOK ROOMS.

the titles, numbers, and other marks on the backs of the volumes may be easily read.

Windows should therefore be placed in the walls which run at right angles to the bookcases.

The simplest arrangement of windows is that in which the cases either abut against or are opposite to the piers between the windows, the width of the gangways being wholly or partially devoted to window space (Figs. 43 and 44).

If such an arrangement does not allow a sufficient width for the windows, they can be so spaced that every other case corresponds with a pier (Figs. 45 and 46).

Where the lighting is chiefly from above, the spacing of the vertical windows, if there are any, need not of necessity correspond with that of the cases, though it is obvious that without such a correspondence a considerable proportion of the window area may be rendered ineffective.

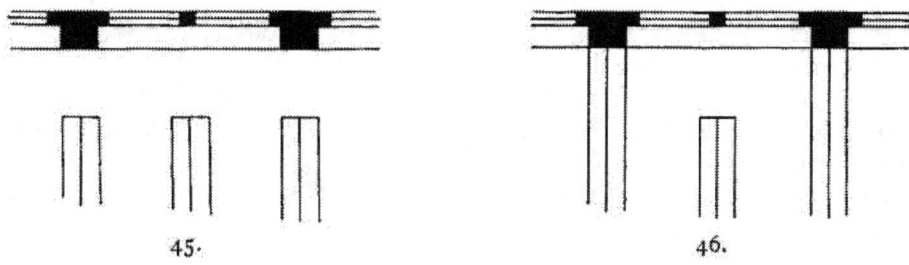

45.   46.

One other arrangement of shelving in a book room must be noticed, namely the system in which the floor-cases radiate from a central space which is usually occupied by a staff enclosure (*cf.* Figs. 77 and 88, pp. 130 and 141). The obvious disadvantage of this system is the waste of space it involves; for, provided that the gangways between the cases are of a sufficient width at the ends nearest the centre, an ever-increasing waste must occur towards their other extremities. This may be to some extent remedied by inserting intermediate lines of radiating cases where the gangways are of sufficient width.

In the case of British public libraries, where the necessity for every economy is so instant, the objection on the score of wastefulness is possibly more serious than it is in America where the system originated.

The primary object of this disposition was to increase the facilities for supervision in book rooms open to the public. The sacrifice of space is, however, disproportionate to the gain, and the idea is illustrative of the common tendency to over-estimate the value of police methods in public libraries. A more justifiable occasion for its use is in book rooms to which the public are not admitted, and in which its adoption facilitates a speedy service by allowing direct access to every part of the shelving, and in open libraries too something is gained in respect of accessibility.

Book rooms shelved on this system are usually semicircular on plan, which is certainly not a recommendation where economy in cost is of prime importance.

Stacks and Stack Rooms.—It has already been pointed out that, in order to keep all the shelves in a book room within reach without the use of ladders, either the cases must not exceed 7 ft. 8 in. in height or some form of gallery must be provided.

Where the cases in a book room are arranged as has been described above, it is obvious that galleries over the narrow gangways will practically form a floor, in that they will occupy almost the whole space between the cases.

When a large number of books have to be accommodated on a comparatively small area, several such floors, or more properly decks, at intervals of from 7 to 8 ft., may be provided; so that by the addition of one story above the lower tier of cases, the accommodation of the area will be doubled, by two trebled, and so on.

This is known as the stack system, and though not required by the municipal workshop library, it must nevertheless be described, since it is the only satisfactory method of accommodating big stocks, as for instance in a large reference library.

There are in existence stacks containing as many as nine tiers of cases, but it is obvious that without a quick and adequate lift-service, every flight of stairs which has to be climbed not only delays service but puts a very considerable physical strain upon the attendants. Generally speaking, no stack should be of such a height as to involve the use of more than two or at most two and a half flights of stairs for access to any part of the shelving; unless, as has been said, the work is on a scale sufficient to justify the institution of a thoroughly efficient lift-service.

A maximum of two flights of stairs does not, however, imply the limitation of a stack to two tiers of cases, but to five; since the stack can be arranged with three book-stories above and two below the floor on which the books are required (Fig. 47).

BOOK ROOMS.

In the same way, with a stack of three tiers, one flight up and one down will suffice.

Where the number of tiers is even, the levels at which the books are to be delivered may be half-way between two decks of the stack (Fig. 48). By this method one and a half flights each way will give access to four, and two and a half to six tiers of cases.

In many situations it is, of course, impossible to economise quite

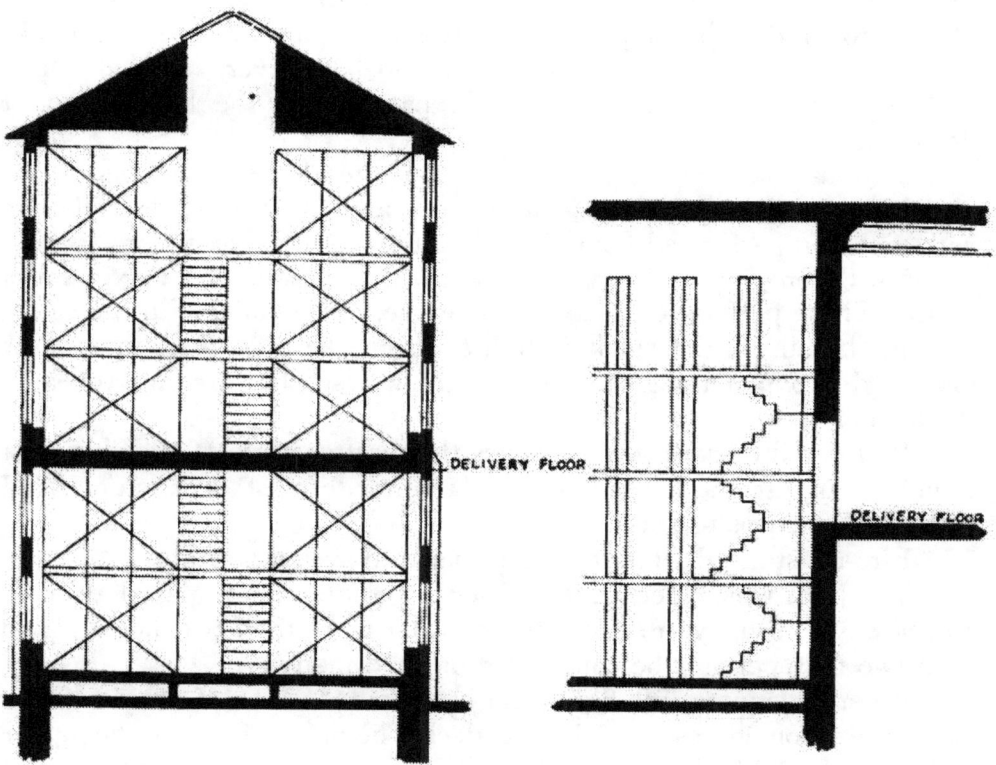

47. SECTION OF BOOK STACK WITH FIVE TIERS OF CASES.

48. SECTION OF BOOK STACK WITH FOUR TIERS OF CASES.

as closely as this, but, where stairs have to be used, their number should always be reduced to a minimum.

Book stacks are so constructed that the cases themselves support the decks and the superimposed tiers; the walls merely serving to keep out the weather, to support the roof, and, to a certain extent, to steady the whole structure.

The decks should be so constructed as to allow of a free circulation of light and air, and to waste as little height as possible.

It is, however, advisable that there should be a solid floor under at least every three tiers of cases, as a protection in case of fire.

In order to facilitate inter-communication between the stories, and to gain the maximum diffusion of light, air, and heat, and also to afford facilities for running pipes, tubes, and wires up and down the stack, the decks are usually stopped at a distance of 3 or 4 in. short of the faces of the shelving on either side. The space thus left should be protected by a flange and a low rail, which also serves as a step. They should also be covered with hemp or wire netting, or gauze, to prevent books from falling through. Openings should, however, be left here and there through which books and papers may be handed up or down.

Various materials are employed for the decks of stacks. The construction is nearly always iron or steel, and often they are filled in with cast-iron perforated flooring. The best form of cast-iron flooring is one with long perforations, which allow the passage of a maximum of light. These perforations should, of course, run parallel with the cases, not only because if the stack is lighted from the side they thus allow more light to penetrate, but because transverse slits are apt to catch the toes of boots.

Perforated decks have, however, the disadvantage of allowing dust to fall through to the lower tiers, and a better form of deck is one filled with roughened plate glass.

Fire-resisting glass is sometimes used in such a position.

The light which permeates either a perforated or glazed deck is not, however, usually effective after passing more than two floors; and even two may perhaps be considered one too many.

Where adequate side-lights can be obtained, slabs of slate or white marble are sometimes used in the decks, being rubbed on the upper surface and polished on the soffit. White marble gives a very good diffusion of light.

A deck in a book stack need not generally be thicker than 4 in. over all, and consequently a spacing of 16 ft. 10 in. or 7 ft. floor to floor gives ample head room. Where spaces are left between the decks and the shelves the books on the top shelf of a tier may if necessary project slightly above the soffit of the deck above.

The staircases in book stacks are usually of iron, and should be fitted with indiarubber treads. The flights should be straight and not spiral, and generally there should be no winders. Proper hand-rails should be provided. The steps may be formed with 8-in. risers and 9-in treads.

BOOK ROOMS.

Book-lifts are of course most necessary where the stack system is used, and in large stacks there should be one or more lifts of a size sufficient to take two or three persons and a number of books.

Stairs and lifts should always be placed as near as possible either to the entrances or to the spot to which the books are to be brought.

It is also important that there should be communication by means of speaking-tubes or telephones* between the different tiers and the floor on which the librarian or other members of the staff are chiefly engaged.

With regard to the lighting of stack rooms, the limit of efficiency of light passing downward through the decks of a stack has already been mentioned. Similarly, with regard to the diffusion of light horizontally, it has been found that, in a stack with narrow gangways, the light from side windows becomes inefficient at a greater distance than about 20 ft. from the glass.

Thus a stack lighted from one side only must not be more than about 20 ft. wide *plus* the width of a passage against the far wall; while a stack lighted on both sides should not be much more than 40 ft. *plus* the width of a central passage which, may often be with advantage lighted from above.†

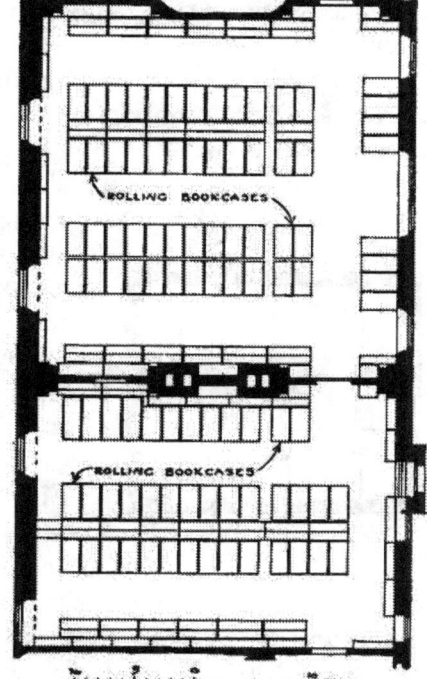

49. PLAN OF BOOK STORE AT THE INDIA OFFICE LIBRARY, LONDON, SHOWING ARRANGEMENT OF ROLLING BOOKCASES.

The windows of stacks are sometimes carried up irrespective of the decks, these being stopped flush with the inner wall face and provided with rails.

Book Stores.—Hitherto the accommodation of such books only

---

* See Chapter III., p. 28.

† Kortum and Schmitt ("Handbuch der Architektur: Bibliotheken," Art. 82), quoting existing examples, give 6 to 7 m. as the width for a stack lighted from one side and 20 m. for one lighted from both. The latter measurement, of course, allows for a considerable central passage with generally a top-light over it.

as are in more or less common use has been considered, in the case of which accessibility is of importance.

Though, as has been already said, "live" books should constitute the main, if not the entire stock of a municipal public library, there are nearly always a certain number of volumes which, while they cannot be altogether abandoned, are yet so seldom asked for that their accessibility is a comparatively unimportant consideration.

In the average public library these would be accommodated in the less accessible parts of the ordinary cases, that is in the top and bottom shelves.

Sometimes, however, and more especially in large reference libraries, their number is so great that some special accommodation becomes necessary.

In such cases, as has been indicated, the need for economy of space assumes a far greater importance than the need of accessibility.

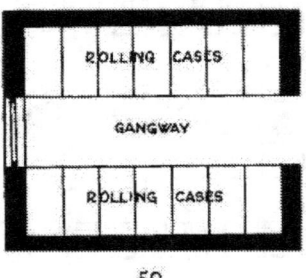

50.

Such an economy may, of course, be obtained by close spacing of the cases, and by carrying these to a considerable height and using ladders for the upper shelves. But a still more economical and at the same time a less inconvenient system is that of rolling bookcases such as have been described above* (Fig. 49).

The simplest form of store-room for the use of this system would be a room 9 ft. wide with a row of rolling cases standing endwise against each of the side walls and leaving a 3-ft. gangway in the centre, into which any case would be rolled from which a book was to be taken. If the cases were carried to the full height of the ceiling practically two-thirds of the whole cubic capacity of the room would be devoted to books (Fig. 50).

These rolling cases can be arranged on the stack system, though, of course the decks must occupy more space than those described above, since they have to be of sufficient strength to support the rolling cases and have to provide rails for the rollers.

Owing to their very occasional use artificial light is all that need be provided in book stores. They are therefore often placed in basements, and electric light can be obtained for them at a cheap rate.†

---

* Chapter IV., pp. 38 and 39.   † See Chapter II., p. 16.

Heating is also unnecessary, though dryness and thorough ventilation are most essential.

Store-Rooms for Files of Periodicals.—Files of periodicals are often accommodated in a very rough and ready manner in the general store-rooms.

Where special rooms are provided for this purpose, the best method is to fit them with open racks, such as have been already mentioned,* both against the walls and on the floor.

Librarians differ as to the details of arrangement, but as a very usual system, that of placing the racks for magazines and the smaller periodicals round the walls, and those for large newspapers in the centre, may be mentioned.

The requirements of these rooms in respect of lighting, heating, and ventilation, do not differ from those of book stores.

---

* Chapter IV., p. 38, and Chapter V., p. 43.

Chapter VII.

LENDING DEPARTMENT.

As has been already indicated, the lending out of books has become a very prominent feature of public library work, and the space assigned to this department usually forms one of the most important sections of the building.

The question between barriers and open shelves has an important bearing on lending libraries, and these may be considered to fall, as regards planning and arrangement generally, into two distinct classes according as the one system or the other is adopted.

Barrier System.

General.—Where the public are not admitted to the shelves, the lending department falls into two distinct sections: the first, that to which the public are admitted, and where they consult catalogues, apply for the books they require, and wait while these are brought to them by the staff: the second, that in which the books are stored. This section, again, is capable of a further subdivision, space being required not only for the bookcases themselves, but for the staff who are engaged in the business of the department.

As to the first of these sections, the space for the public must be, above all things, roomy, light, and well ventilated.

There are always certain hours which borrowers find more convenient than others in which to visit a library, and into these periods a large proportion of the day's work in the lending department is always crowded. Consequently in the planning of lending libraries the accommodation for borrowers must be calculated, not from the average of visits throughout the day, but from the number to be expected during "flush" times; for confusion among the borrowers is entirely fatal to a rapid service.

Occasionally the borrowers' space forms part of an entrance hall, sometimes even of a reading room. The former arrangement may be satisfactory, provided the space be sufficiently ample to avoid congestion; but when borrowers have to share a 10-ft. corridor with those entering and leaving other departments, the result is too often chaos.

The other combination, that of borrowers' space and reading room, is entirely objectionable. Even where the two departments are separated by a barrier, disturbance to the readers is inevitable.

A good light is also essential, more especially where catalogues or indicators have to be consulted, or application forms filled in; while during the "flush" times the need for ventilation is only too often noticeable.

There remains to be considered the accommodation for staff and books.

The duties of the attendants in a barrier lending library are very various. Not only have they to charge issues and discharge returns, and to carry books to and from the shelves, but they must demand and receive fines, issue application forms and tickets, answer queries, and generally help and advise borrowers. Moreover, it is always uncertain at what particular moment the full complement of attendants may be required. The library may be at one minute quite empty of borrowers and full the next. Thus, for a considerable part of the day, some, if not all, of the attendants, who nevertheless cannot be allowed to absent themselves from the lending library, would perforce be idle were they not provided with sufficient space to enable them to carry on such work as cataloguing and repairing in the lending library itself. It is also usual, especially where the staff is large, to provide a desk near the counter where a sub-librarian or superior attendant can work and be always at hand to assist and direct borrowers and attendants.

A roomy and well-lighted working space for the staff, though often conspicuously absent, is therefore an essential feature of the lending department. The requirements of book rooms of various forms having been fully dealt with above, it remains to consider the relative disposition and general arrangement of the three sections into which the department has been divided.

It is obvious that in any barrier library the only possible arrangement is that which places the working space for the staff between the borrowers' space and the bookcases. The barrier itself will, of course, be placed between the public and staff, and always consists wholly or in part of a counter, at which the transfer of volumes and other business connected therewith is conducted.

The requirements of this counter differ according as indicators are used or not, and the arrangement of the whole department is thereby affected. Consequently indicator lending libraries will be next considered, and then those in which ledgers or cards are the only system of charging employed.

Barrier System—with Indicators.—The most important item in the planning of an indicator lending library is the counter, which has to be of sufficient length to accommodate the indicators, showcases, and sometimes catalogues, and to provide spaces for the issue and return of volumes, for the payment of fines, and for inquiries. Different forms of indicator require, as has been said, different lengths of counter for the registration of a given number of volumes, and it is, of course, essential to know, before planning a lending library, the form of indicator to be accommodated and the number of volumes to

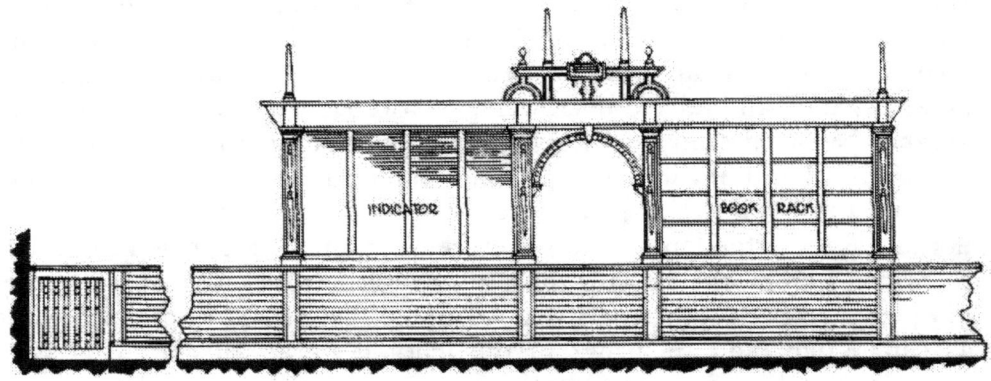

51. INDICATOR SCREEN, WAKEFIELD PUBLIC LIBRARY.
Alfred Cox, F.R.I.B.A, *Architect.*

be registered thereby; and the requisite length of counter will, of course, be considerably greater than that required for the transfer of books only.

Indeed, in a library with a large stock, and where the whole of this is registered on indicators, the arrangement of the long counter required often becomes a difficult problem, while an increase of stock may mean that the whole department has to be remodelled.

As a matter of fact the provision of indicators for the whole stock would seem to be quite unnecessary, and where they are used for fiction only the indicator space is reduced by about 67 per cent.

The height of the counter should not, as has been said, exceed about 2 ft. 6 in., or the numbers near the tops of the indicators will not be easily read by children and short persons. The indicators are

LENDING DEPARTMENT.

placed near the front of the counter, a ledge being left behind on which returned books and other articles may be temporarily placed. The unsightly appearance of the indicators may be to some extent cloaked by setting them in a screen (Fig. 51) placed on the counter. The greatest care must be taken to secure a good light throughout this department, and particularly on both sides of the indicators.

The borrowers' space is only too often very narrow and inconvenient. Attempts have been made to prevent confusion by means of barriers, but any complicated system of sorting borrowers, unless the attendants were to devote their whole time to shepherding them, would inevitably lead to more complete chaos. The depth in front of the counter should not generally be less than 10 and, better still, 12 ft., more especially if this space is used as a passage to any other public room (see Fig. 79, p. 132).

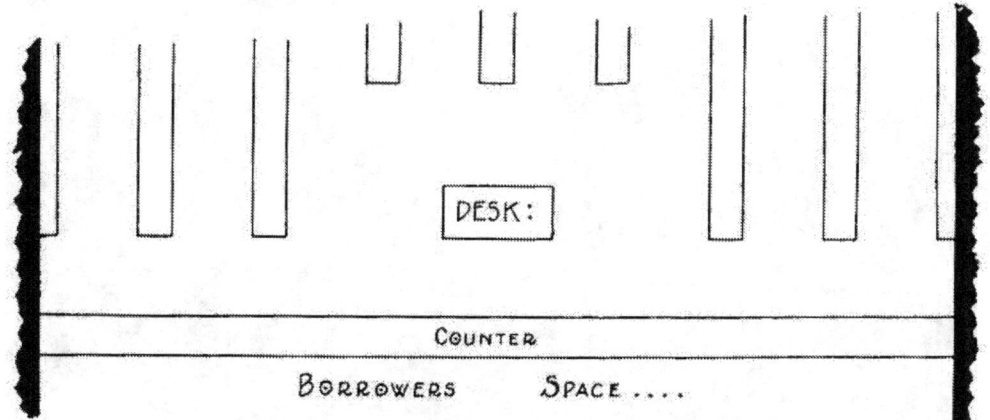

52. Lending Library Counter showing space left for Staff.

Great care is necessary in so disposing indicators or catalogues that there shall be no fear of congestion in internal angles of the counter.

Economy of time in issuing books is of the greatest importance, and the gangways between the bookcases should run, if possible, at right angles to the counter, while in large libraries, where the distances are considerable, each indicator should be near the shelves containing the volumes registered by it.

The ends of the bookcases should be brought as close to the counter as possible, a space of 3 ft. being usually sufficient. Where, however, there is no other working space for the staff in close proximity to the counter this must be obtained by setting the ends of a few of the cases well back (Fig. 52).

Barrier System—without Indicators.—The real object of the indicator is to enable readers and staff to ascertain whether a book is in or out without having to search the shelves.

With a very small daily issue not exceeding, say, three hundred volumes, it is usually considered safe to depend upon the memory of an attendant, while, where the system of card charging is employed, the presence or absence of any particular volume can be automatically registered at the counter. Consequently the only advantage left which can be claimed by the indicator is that it saves the attendants from frequent interrogation.

53. Delivery Counter, Massachusetts State Library.

Whether such an immunity is sufficient compensation for the disadvantages, it is for the librarian to decide; and certainly a very large section of the world's librarians have answered in the negative. From the architectural point of view, indeed, a reduction of the length of the counter enables the lending department to be planned on an altogether more desirable system.

The best patterns for barrier libraries without indicators, owing to their scarcity in this country, are to be found in America, where the indicator has never been assimilated.

LENDING DEPARTMENT.

The two main sections and the subdivision into which the lending department has been divided, namely, the spaces for borrowers, books, and staff, may, with the abolition of the long counter, be realised in the plan itself; that is to say, the borrowers' space becomes one separate room, and often the working space for the staff a second, and the book room a third. The staff space, which takes the form of a workroom, often with other workrooms opening out of it, is placed, of course, between the book room and the borrowers' space (which is known in America as the delivery room), and communicates on the one hand with the book room, on the other with the borrowers' space, from which it is separated by the counter or issue desk (see Fig. 70, p. 125).

This plan has many advantages over that of dividing up one large room.

In the first place, in the winter time the delivery room and workroom require a much higher temperature than is necessary for the books, and if the book room is separated from these a great economy may be effected in respect of heating.

54. DELIVERY ROOM, MILWAUKEE (WIS.) PUBLIC LIBRARY.

Moreover, this method makes possible the adoption of the stack system, while the stack, being hidden from the public gaze, may be as plain and inexpensive as possible.

Lastly, a good workroom can be provided for the staff immediately behind the counter, and for the borrowers a dignified and even luxurious hall (Figs. 53 and 54).

In America the delivery room usually forms the central vestibule of the building, giving access to the reading rooms. It usually errs, if at all, in the direction of too great liberality of space, while it is generally fitted with comfortable seats, catalogue cabinets, and tables; though sometimes a separate catalogue room adjoins it.

The best form of counter is one which curves outward into the delivery room, and gives a greater length on the public than on the staff side. A height of about 3 ft. is generally recommended.

Of course in America there is more money available for purposes of library building than here, and the examples adduced are no doubt on a more lordly scale than can often be attempted in England, nor are they all taken from municipal libraries.

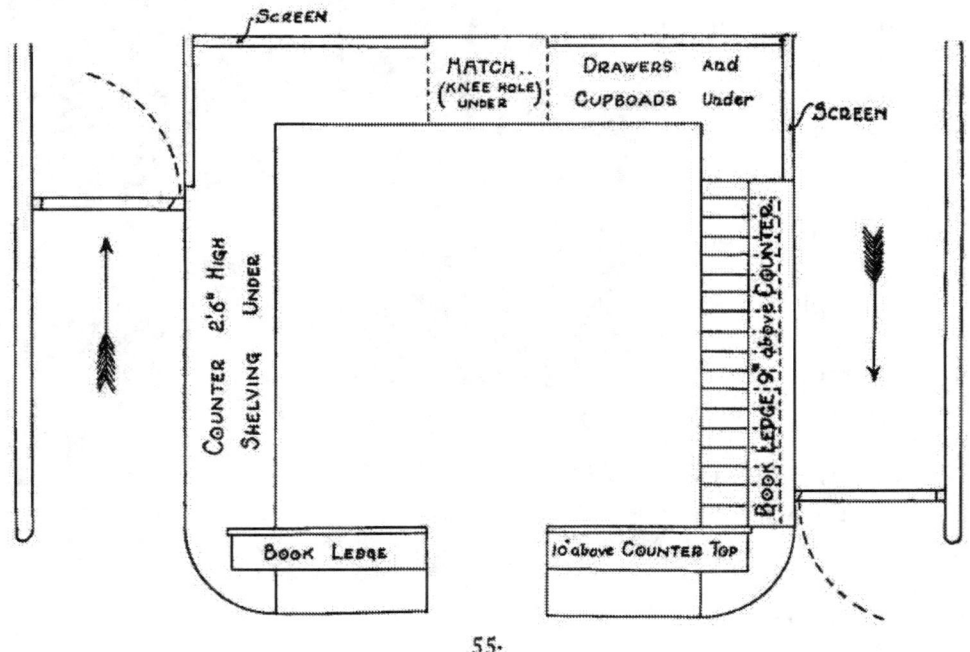

55.

Open Access System.

Open Shelf System.—The form of open access which seems likely to become common in the lending departments of British libraries is more accurately described as safeguarded open access. Where this system is adopted, it is not, as in some American libraries, left practically to the choice of the borrower whether he registers his loan or not. On the contrary, he can only enter the library by returning a book previously borrowed, or by showing his ticket, and can only leave it when another book has been charged and his ticket left in pledge.

56. Staff Enclosure, Kettering Public Library. *Messrs Goddard & Sons, Architects.*

LENDING DEPARTMENT.

The logical division of the open shelf library is essentially different from that of the barrier library: the one section being in this case the accommodation for the staff, the other that for readers and books.

From what has been said above it will be obvious that the staff accommodation must be near both entrance and exit to the book store.

Usually it takes the form of an enclosure (Fig. 55) with an inside dimension of not less than 6 ft. by 10 ft., since, as in barrier libraries, the staff space must be used for miscellaneous work during slack times.

At one end of this enclosure is the entrance to the book room, at the other the exit (Figs. 56 and 57).

57. STAFF ENCLOSURE TO LENDING LIBRARY, KINGSTON PUBLIC LIBRARY.
Alfred Cox, F.R.I.B.A., *Architect.*

It is a great advantage for an attendant, whether charging or discharging, to have only one borrower at a time at the service space, and consequently both those entering and those leaving the library should be marshalled into single file. This is done by making both entrance and exit in the form of gangways not more than 2 ft. wide, each gangway having at the end a wicket opened by a treadle latch worked from inside the counter. This gives the attendants complete control over borrowers arriving and leaving.

Between the entrance and exit gangways and the working space for the staff counters not less than 2 ft. wide should be provided. This gives space for service and for the accommodation of charging trays. On the side towards the book room the counter should be returned, but with an opening 2 ft. 6 in. wide in the centre for the passage of a third attendant, who will be occupied during busy times in carrying returned books from the staff enclosure to the shelves. The remaining side should also be provided with a counter for returned books, extra trays, and apparatus generally.

In order to charge and discharge as quickly and easily as possible an attendant must have the trays on his left-hand side, and it should never be necessary to turn round to reach them. This may be secured by putting the entrance on the left, looking from the enclosure towards the book room (Fig. 55). The parts of the counter used for the trays should be protected by a low wire screen, while the side away from the book room may be protected in the same way or by a high glazed screen, where necessary an opening being usually provided for inquiries (Fig. 56). It is, of course, preferable that the entrance and exit gangways should not have doors at the ends, but should either be open to the entrance vestibule (Fig. 56) or to a wider corridor within the lending library itself (Fig. 57).

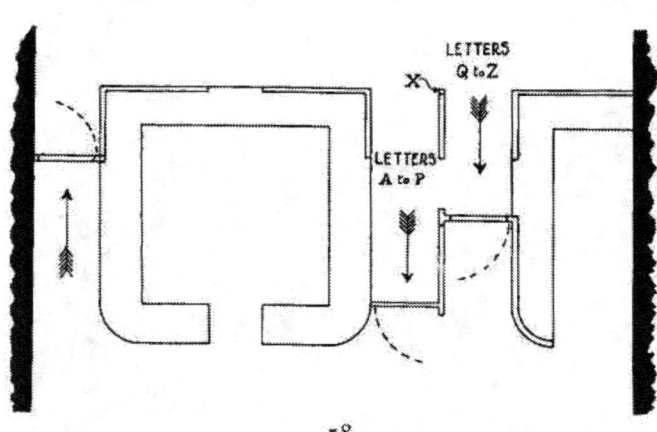

58.

Such a staff enclosure with one entrance and one exit wicket, and worked by three attendants, will easily suffice for an issue of say 1,000 volumes a day. Where, however, the issue reaches 1,400 or 1,500 volumes, the work will be found to be beyond their capacity and some new arrangement must be adopted. One method of meeting such an increase is to divide the borrowers into two classes according to their initials. For each class a separate entrance wicket and a separate attendant is necessary (Fig. 58).

As regards the exit, books can be charged and readers despatched so quickly that it is doubtful whether two wickets are essential, though these may be provided if there is space. This arrangement would, how-

LENDING DEPARTMENT.

ever, have the disadvantage of making a double set of book-cards, if not indispensable, at any rate desirable, and as it would require not only more space but an extra attendant, it would be best if possible to avoid it.

The double system, is of course, put into practice only during busy times, the use of either wicket for either class or both being notified by a placard fixed between the wickets.

A good arrangement would be to separate the two classes before they reach the service space by a low barrier, as shown in the illustration, another placard being displayed at the outer end of this. An opening would, however, have to be left opposite the service space in order to obviate the necessity of borrowers having to return after entering the wrong gangway (see Fig. 58).

Inside the entrance wicket accommodation must be provided for catalogues and show-cases. An excellent plan is to provide a separate catalogue room near the entrance wicket, an arrangement which will be dealt with below.*

Where the catalogues have to be actually in the lending library, it is not recommended that they should be placed on the counter, as it is important that as much of this as possible should be left free for staff purposes. They should, however, be placed as near as possible to the counter in order that the staff may give assistance to those consulting them, and it is well, if space be available, that tables and chairs should be provided close to the catalogues and also to the show-case, so that a visitor, in the one instance, may consult the cards in one drawer without blocking those near it: in the other, examine the new books from the show-case before deciding what to borrow.

Further, as has been said in connection with barrier libraries, a desk should usually be provided for a superior attendant in the book room, but in such a position that he is accessible to the staff within the enclosure as well as to the public.

The arrangement of the bookcases is a most important consideration in an open-shelf lending library. Generally speaking, the gangways should run directly away from the staff enclosure to facilitate supervision, while sometimes the American plan of radiating cases is adopted† (see Figs. 77 and 78, pp. 130 and 141).

Shelf classification, which assumes great importance where the public are admitted to the shelves, is really a question for librarians rather than for architects. It must, however, be remembered that

---

* Chapter X., pp. 99-101.
† This is discussed above, Chapter VI., pp. 63 and 64.

some classes, prose fiction for instance, are more apt to attract crowds than others, and a good deal may be done by a judicious distribution of the different classes to ensure the free circulation of the borrowers.

It is important, too, that the position of any class should be readily recognisable. This can be ensured by the use of conspicuous placards, while a key-plan of the shelves should always be placed near the catalogues.

A good light on the shelves is, of course, very important, and vertical windows should be carried as high as possible in order that borrowers may not get in one another's light.

Conclusion.—Such, then, are the different methods employed in the lending departments of public libraries, and it is the business of the librarian and not of the architect to choose between them.

Sometimes a combination of the barrier system with open shelves has been tried, the former for fiction, the latter for the other classes. This necessitates the separation of the one class from the rest of the stock ; nor, once the principle of open access is recognised, does there seem any necessity to complicate the work of the department by such a compromise.

Chapter VIII.

READING ROOMS.

General.—For reading of any kind, quiet and light are above all things necessary.

Freedom from disturbance, though to some extent secured by the avoidance of resonant floors and such constructional details, must, in the main, be compassed by a judicious disposition of the building generally, and a purposeful arrangement of the reading rooms themselves.

That is to say, not only should the reading accommodation be isolated as completely as possible from the traffic of entrances, lending libraries, and so on; but the tables or desks in the rooms themselves should be so placed that any one may pass to or from any seat without disturbing those actually at work. To this end a liberal allowance of space is, of course, essential, and in no circumstances should the desire to provide accommodation for the greatest possible number of readers be allowed, as it only too often is, to result in overcrowding, since it is surely preferable that a few should be enabled to do profitable work than that many should be accommodated under conditions which make serious study impossible. Economy of space is, however, as has been already said, of the greatest importance, and in so far as such economy can be furthered by the purposeful disposition of the fittings and furniture in reading rooms, this consideration must, of course, be allowed full weight.

This question of the disposition of the furniture is conditioned not only by the nature of the furniture itself, but more especially by the shape of the room and the distribution of the light.

Thus, in ordinary rectangular rooms, if the lighting is from vertical windows, the reading tables or desks should be placed at right angles to the walls in which such windows occur, so that the light is thrown lengthwise from the ends of the tables and no reader is hampered by his own shadow or by a light directly in his eyes. In such rooms, if the tables or desks are used for writing as well as for reading, it is important that the strongest light should come from the left. Generally it is quite sufficient if half the seats at each table give this advantage, and therefore double tables with readers seated on each side are generally used (Fig. 59). In special cases, however, single

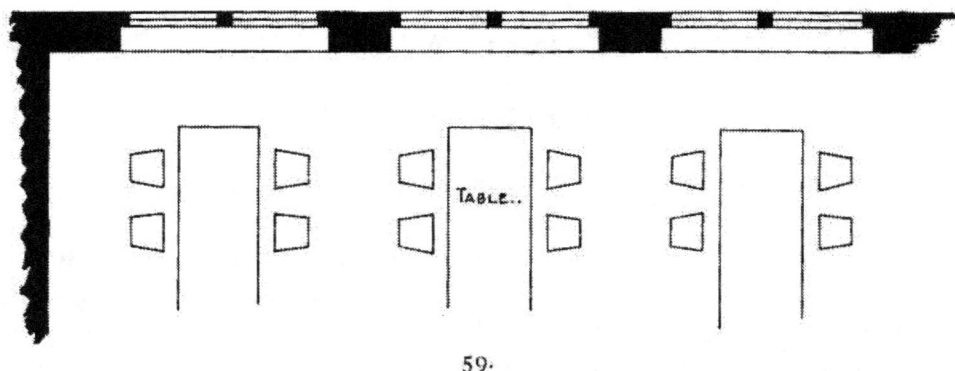

59.

desks or tables with seats on one side only are preferred (Fig. 60). When such are used in a room lighted from both sides, the desks in each half of the room may face the reverse way to those in the other, so that each set of tables may get the strongest light from the left. In very large rooms, lighted from one side and one or both ends, it is

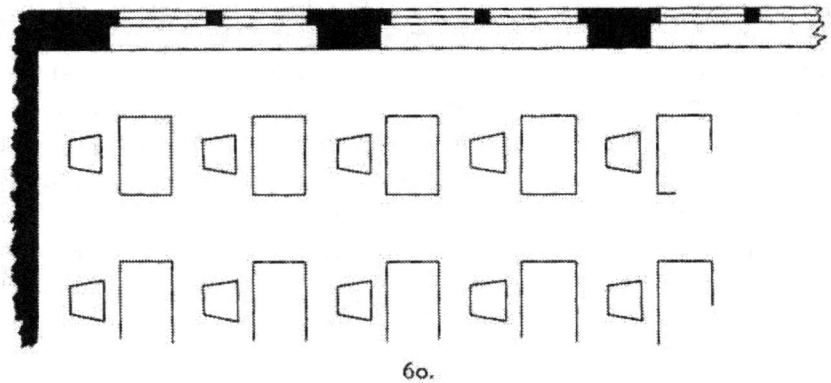

60.

sometimes desirable, in order to avoid shadows, that the desks or tables at the ends of the rooms should be placed at right angles to the end walls, though this method involves a considerable waste of space.

Where the space and light are both ample, the disposition of the tables need not of necessity follow that of the windows, though such an arrangement is, of course, in many ways preferable. Where the tables have to be brought near to the wall, or where the sills are high, the tables should be placed directly opposite the windows, and the sills must be sufficiently splayed to prevent their shadow from falling on the tables.

In the same way, if the tables are placed opposite the piers, the jambs must be bevelled sufficiently to allow the light to be thrown on the ends of the tables nearest the wall.

In the case of rooms which are lighted from above the arrangement of the furniture is not bound by any of these conditions, and can follow more freely the dictates of convenience and economy.

As has been indicated above, it is most important that the disposition of the furniture should be such that a reader after entering the room or obtaining books from a counter may be able to reach any seat without disturbing those already at work. This must depend, of course, to a large extent on the position of the room in relation to the other parts of the building, the entrances, counters, and so on. In every case, however, liberal passage room and frequent cross-gangways are essential to easy and direct traffic. The actual dimensions of the gangways will, of course, vary according to the kind of reading for which any particular room is intended. That is to say, in rooms devoted to especially studious work freedom from disturbance is more essential, and a more liberal spacing is therefore necessary, than in rooms used solely for magazine reading.

No doubt a spacing which results in an allowance of 50 sq. ft. per reader, such as is sometimes found in American reading rooms, is to be admired, but, under the conditions prevailing in this country, such liberality would be nothing short of extravagance, and 24 to 25 sq. ft. must be considered a very ample allowance.*

The amount of table space required for each reader has already been dealt with above,† and there remains to be considered the width of the passages between the tables and that of the cross-gangways at their ends. It may be safely affirmed that in the case of double tables or desks the space between, which has to accommodate two rows of seats and at the same time provide passage room, should in no circumstances be less than 5 ft., and, where movable chairs are used, 6 ft. should be considered a minimum. Indeed, even a 6-ft. passage should only be considered sufficient where the tables are short and the passage intended solely for access to the seats on either side of it. Where such passages are intended to give access to any other part of

---

* See Chapter III., p. 22. † Chapter V., pp. 44-48.

the room, the space should be increased to, at the very least, 7 ft.; and this again may have to be increased proportionately to the amount of the traffic.

With single tables or desks a space of 3 ft. may be considered sufficient for access to the seats only, provided always that the desks are in short lengths with frequent cross-gangways; but this again, as with the double tables, may have to be increased.

For cross-gangways intended merely for the purpose of allowing persons to pass on occasion, a space of 2 ft. is sufficient between the ends of the tables and the walls, and 2 ft. 6 in. or 3 ft. between one table and another; but this must be increased to 4 ft. if intended for anything like regular traffic.

Where circular and oval tables are used (see Fig. 74, p. 129) the spacing is of necessity very liberal, and it is unnecessary to fix any rigid dimensions.

No general remarks on reading rooms would be complete without some brief mention of those of circular and semicircular form, though their desirability in the case of municipal public libraries is more than doubtful.

Circular reading rooms are often lighted from above, and consequently the disposition of the tables is not dictated by that of windows.

Vertical windows, however, give a very good diffused light in a circular or semicircular room. No special tables need be used, though their arrangement needs care (see Fig. 78, p. 130).

If a circular reading room is used largely for periodical reading, it is, of course, better to use a few small tables of the ordinary type very liberally spaced (see Fig. 73, p. 128).

Reading Rooms for Periodicals.

Under the present head will be discussed, in the first instance, those rooms in which the daily and weekly periodicals are provided: in the second, rooms for the accommodation of readers of magazines, monthly and quarterly.

Often one room serves both these purposes, and a few remarks on this combination will be appended.

Newspaper Reading Rooms. — In this country the newspaper reading rooms form a much more considerable feature of public libraries than elsewhere, and, if judged by the amount spent on them in respect

61. NEWSPAPER READING ROOM, KETTERING PUBLIC LIBRARY.

Messrs Goddard & Sons, Architects.

of site, fabric, and furnishing, in maintenance and provision of literature, would often appear to be the most important section of the institution. How far the educational value of daily and weekly newspapers balances the expense, often nearly a third of the whole cost of the library, and how far the abolition, or at least the reduction, of this department is desirable or possible, is, as has been said, a question which the librarian and the library authority can alone decide.

The literature provided in a room such as we are considering falls into two classes: the first, the ordinary daily broadsheet: the second, the weekly papers, illustrated and otherwise, the technical journals, and so on.

The method of accommodating the daily papers on reading slopes has already been mentioned and the fittings described (Chapter V., pp. 48-50).

The space occupied by the newspaper slopes themselves is considerable, and they further require very liberal spacing. When double stands are used, the gangways between them should be never less than 6 ft., and 6 ft. 6 in. is preferable. Consequently, with stands 2 ft. 6 in. wide the minimum spacing, centre to centre, should be 8 ft. 6 in.

Wall slopes, however, as has been already stated, are far superior, since they cause less interruption to supervision as well as to ventilation, and also because the whereabouts of any particular paper can be seen at once by any one entering the room.

Where used, double slopes should, of course, unless the room is top-lighted, be placed at right angles to the walls in which the windows occur (Fig. 61).

It is an advantage if the direction of the gangways is such that they can be easily scanned by the staff.

Wall slopes, except in top-lighted rooms, should be placed under the sills, the height of which will have to be not less than 6 ft. above the floor. Windows over slopes should always be provided with blinds which can be rolled upward from the sill to keep the glare out of the eyes of the readers on bright days. Indeed it is an advantage to keep the sills slightly above the eyes of the readers, and a height of 6 ft. 6 in. or even 7 ft. is desirable.

If double slopes are used, it is best that they should be placed in the part of the room nearest to the entrance, since there is usually more coming and going among the readers of daily papers than among the others, and this arrangement, therefore, involves least disturbance to the latter (see Fig. 75).

Where, on the other hand, wall slopes are adopted, the readers of weekly papers and technical journals will occupy the centre of the room (Fig. 62).

In this case it is most important that ample space should be left between the reading slopes and the tables or desks, more especially since with this arrangement a good deal of the traffic is apt to follow the newspaper slopes round the walls. An absolute minimum should

62. NEWSPAPER READING ROOM, KINGSTON PUBLIC LIBRARY.

Alfred Cox, A.R.I.B.A., *Architect.*

be considered to be 7 ft. where seats have to be accommodated, and 4 ft. or 4 ft. 6 in. at the ends of tables.

For readers of weekly papers and others reading tables or slopes such as those already described are provided, and the rules governing the disposition of such furniture have already been given.*

With regard to the methods of displaying these forms of periodical,

---

* Pages 83 and 84.

whether they are to be kept loose on the tables, or in table racks, or tied down, or whether they are to be placed in wall racks, is another of those questions which must be left to the librarians. The architect must, however, be prepared to provide accommodation for whatever fittings may be required in any particular instance, including racks for time-tables, newspaper files, and so on. Not infrequently, certain periodicals are not displayed in the reading room, but are produced on application to an attendant. Where this is the case a short counter, from 3 to 10 ft. long according to circumstances, should be provided, as near as possible to the entrance to the room, with, if necessary, a box for an attendant and accommodation for the retained periodicals. It is, of course, a great advantage, if possible, for this counter to adjoin the lending library or some place where there are attendants continually employed.

Magazine Reading Rooms. — The accommodation for magazine readers does not necessarily differ materially from that required by readers of weekly papers. The methods of displaying them are similar and equally numerous; and in each case the space must be calculated to accommodate such fittings as the system adopted may require. As has been mentioned above, some librarians prefer to keep magazines behind a barrier and let them out on application; an indicator, already described, being used to show which are in and which out.

This method certainly avoids the confusion which is inevitable, when the readers are requested never so earnestly to replace them in the racks or even to leave them on the tables, while the disadvantages of tying them to their places are many.

It has already been suggested that a very pleasant arrangement for magazine readers is a rather free disposition of tables and chairs liberally spaced. It is to many persons far more comfortable not to feel bound to sit in any particular position, nor, unless they wish it, close to a table. A magazine reader often prefers to sit in a comfortable chair with a magazine on his knee or held in his hand and, with systematically arranged tables and close spacing, this would involve the blocking of the gangways between. Consequently, as has been suggested above, liberality of floor space is more desirable than the provision of much table space (Fig. 63).

Such a system of furnishing reading rooms is common in America and has been tried in this country with success.

General Periodical Reading Rooms.—Frequently one large room is provided for newspaper and magazine readers together.

In this case the magazine readers will generally be accommodated at the same tables as the readers of weekly newspapers.

Generally it is best, where possible, to place the tables for magazine readers in the quietest part of the room: that is to say, the part most remote from the entrance. Indeed a selection of the more serious magazines is not infrequently housed in the reference reading room, an arrangement which will be further dealt with below.

Often time-tables, gazetteers, directories, and other "quick-reference" books are placed on open shelves in the periodical room.

63. Reference and Reading Room, Carnegie Library, Homestead, U.S.A.

Women's Reading Rooms.—In many libraries special reading rooms have been provided for women only: generally with indifferent success. The truth is, that most of them do not care to be considered as creatures apart.

Where, however, the architect is instructed to provide such a room, he must remember that it is quite a mistake to suppose that privacy is desirable. On the contrary, women's rooms have been found to require more supervision than those in which the presence of the sterner sex acts as a check: mutilation of papers, particularly those containing fashion-plates, being far too common.

The literature provided in such a room consists of weekly papers and magazines, especially, of course, those attractive to the feminine mind, and the furniture required differs in no way from that already recommended for the same classes of literature in other reading rooms.

If public lavatories are provided, that for women should, of course, open from their reading room.

Juvenile Reading Rooms. — Whether children should be separated from adults in public libraries is a question which has provoked a good deal of discussion among librarians, but which is really outside the province of the present work.

In America the children's reading room is a universal and very important item of library accommodation. In this country many libraries provide not only reading accommodation but a special lending department for children.

For juvenile rooms a superficial area of 18 ft. per reader, or even less, may be considered sufficient; and the heights of seats, tables, shelving, and counters should be less than those recommended for adults; while, to some slight extent also, the dimensions of gangways and passages may be reduced.

The furniture and fittings are often cheap, and such as is not damaged by rough usage.

Sometimes juvenile lending libraries are provided, usually in combination with the children's reading rooms; and where girls and boys are separated, the juvenile book store may be placed between the two, so that both sexes may be served by one attendant.

Often there is a separate entrance, and, when the department is on an upper floor, a separate staircase. Such an entrance should be so arranged that it can be thoroughly supervised by the staff, and the same should apply to the staircase, where this is necessary. It is, of course, far preferable that the children should be able to reach their room without having to climb a staircase, and where there is not room for the juvenile accommodation on the ground floor level it is a good plan to place it in a basement or half-basement which may be approached by external steps and a separate entrance. The chief disadvantage of rooms below the ground level is, of course, the difficulty of obtaining daylight, but, since children's rooms in public libraries are chiefly frequented after school hours in the winter evenings when artificial light is necessary, this consideration is not so important in their case as in that of others.

Where stairs are necessary, the risers should not be higher than 6 in., and straight flights without winders are desirable. There should be not less than eight or more than fourteen steps without a landing. Long flights are obviously dangerous; while short flights tempt children to jump instead of descending step by step.

Some authorities recommend box stairs, others open staircases with balusters. Continuous grilles or high balustrades are, however, safe, and do not interfere with supervision. Wooden hand-rails should always be provided, and sometimes, if the ages of the children vary much, that is to say, if the age limit of the adult rooms is high, two hand-rails at different heights, one below the other, are recommended. If boys and girls are to use separate reading rooms, it would appear only logical that they should be provided with separate staircases. Indeed, when the juvenile rooms are at the top of the building, there should always be two good staircases for use in case of fire.

The supervision of boys' and girls' reading rooms, staircases, and entrances is most important, since, when separate juvenile accommodation is provided, the want of the restraining presence of their elders is noticeable.

With regard to the furniture of juvenile rooms, the heights of such fittings as counters, chairs, tables, and so on, depend, of course, to a large extent upon the age limit below which children are excluded from the adult rooms.

The following table,* compiled for the use of schools, gives the approximate heights of desks or tables for readers of varying ages. This, of course, must only be taken as a basis for suggestion, as children vary greatly in growth and height.

Age.	Height of Seat.	Height of Table.
Adult	17 in.	30 in.
16-21	$16\frac{1}{4}$,,	29 ,,
12-18	$15\frac{1}{4}$,,	$27\frac{1}{4}$,,
10-15	$14\frac{1}{4}$,,	$25\frac{1}{4}$,,
8-12	$13\frac{1}{4}$,,	23 ,,
5-8	12 ,,	21 ,,

Sometimes, however, a rather greater height of seat in proportion to that of the tables is thought desirable. In the children's room of one American library† tables and chairs of varying heights are used. These are as follows:—

Height of Seat.	Height of Table.
$17\frac{1}{2}$ in.	30 in.
$16\frac{1}{2}$,,	28 ,,
14 ,,	22 ,,

Unless the age limit of the adult rooms is high, it is better to have one height rather than several, since it is difficult to get the small children to sit at the low tables, and the reverse.

---

* See "Modern School Buildings," by F. Clay, p, 60.
† Carnegie Library, Atlanta, Georgia.

At the same time the seats and tables must on no account be too low for the larger children, and it is best to provide furniture of dimensions suitable for these, and to provide cushions to raise the smaller ones, and, what is most important, footstools that they may not have to sit with their legs dangling.

Where open shelves are provided in the children's room they should be kept low, the top of the highest being not more than, say, 4 ft. 6 in.

Children's rooms should be made as attractive and cheerful as possible. Some American libraries, though many think that child-worship is carried to excess in that country, give very good examples of how these rooms should strike the observer (Fig. 64).

64. LOS ANGELES (CAL.) PUBLIC LIBRARY.

Other Reading Rooms. — Besides the rooms already mentioned in this chapter, there are other subdivisions of the reading accommodation to be found in public libraries, noticeably students' and ratepayers' rooms. Of these, the first will be treated in the following chapter, which deals with rooms for reference work and the more serious forms of reading.

Of ratepayers' rooms all that need be said is that, provided the ordinary rooms are decent and well conducted, there is no need for the introduction of invidious privileges which are entirely opposed to the spirit of an institution which is essentially democratic.

Chapter IX.

REFERENCE DEPARTMENT.

ALTHOUGH the advantage of being able to take a volume away for home reading is often considerable, there is nevertheless a large class of readers whose requirements cannot be met by any one or two volumes, and a reading room where they can consult any volume in the library is usually provided. It is in this department that all the more serious study in the library is done, and therefore those conditions specified above as essential to profitable reading must be here more particularly insisted upon. Usually, too, a considerable proportion of the stock of the library is assigned to this department, consisting of such works as are not considered suitable to the lending department, whether because of their size or because their absence would be likely to be inconvenient.

How far and in what manner the stock of the reference library is separated from the rest depends entirely upon the views of the librarian and his methods, and the various arrangements will be discussed below. But whether the main stock is amalgamated with the rest or distinct from it, there always are or should be a certain number of open shelves in the reading room itself to contain the most frequently used works of reference. Generally speaking, the reference, as the lending department, may be divided into two classes, according as the barrier system or open shelves are adopted; and of these the former class will be first considered.

Barrier Reference Libraries.—Barrier reference libraries may be subdivided into two distinct classes, the one in which readers and books occupy the same room, the other in which they do not.

Where readers and books occupy the same room, the public may be kept from the shelves either by locked wire doors on the cases themselves or by barriers placed about 3 ft. in front of them. The use of doors is not recommended, as they cause a good deal of trouble to the attendants who have to get the books, and the barrier is preferable.

This is generally so arranged that an attendant seated at a desk behind a counter, which sometimes itself forms the barrier, may pass behind the barrier to any part of the shelving. For this the most economical arrangement is, of course, that of parallel floor-cases with narrow gangways. At the counter, which should be near the entrance and should have ample space in front of it, readers apply, usually on a signed form, for the books they require. The catalogues are sometimes placed on this counter and should always be near it, as also should be any open shelves, and such fittings as directory-stands and map-cases.

The desks or tables should be so arranged that readers can pass, as directly as possible and without disturbing others, from the counter or open shelves to any seat which may be vacant.

If the plan allows of the counter being served by an attendant in the lending library, this is an economical arrangement and facilitates the fetching of books if any be required from the lending stock. Care must be taken, however, that reference readers are not exposed to disturbance from the coming and going of borrowers.

Where the stock is very large, it is usual to store it entirely apart from the reading room.

In American barrier libraries, where the whole stock of the library is usually stored together in one stack, the reference reading room often opens out of the central delivery room, the reference readers applying for books at the same counter as the borrowers and taking them into the reading room themselves; while sometimes a part of the counter extends to the reference reading room, the books being issued in the room itself.

The former method has the advantage of keeping the inevitably disturbing business of issue, with its accompaniment of queries and explanations, entirely outside the reading room, and further, of abolishing the necessity for two catalogues.

There seems, however, to be an inclination in this country to keep reference readers entirely separate from borrowers, and certainly British librarians would not be so trustful as to adopt some plans which have been adopted on the other side of the Atlantic, and which appear to be specially designed to encourage theft.

Where the whole stock of a library is devoted to reference readers, the reading room will usually take the same position in relation to the staff working space and book room as is occupied by the delivery room in a lending library, though it is best that a lobby or corridor, at any rate partially separated from the reading room itself, should be provided. With such an arrangement it is important that the counter should be

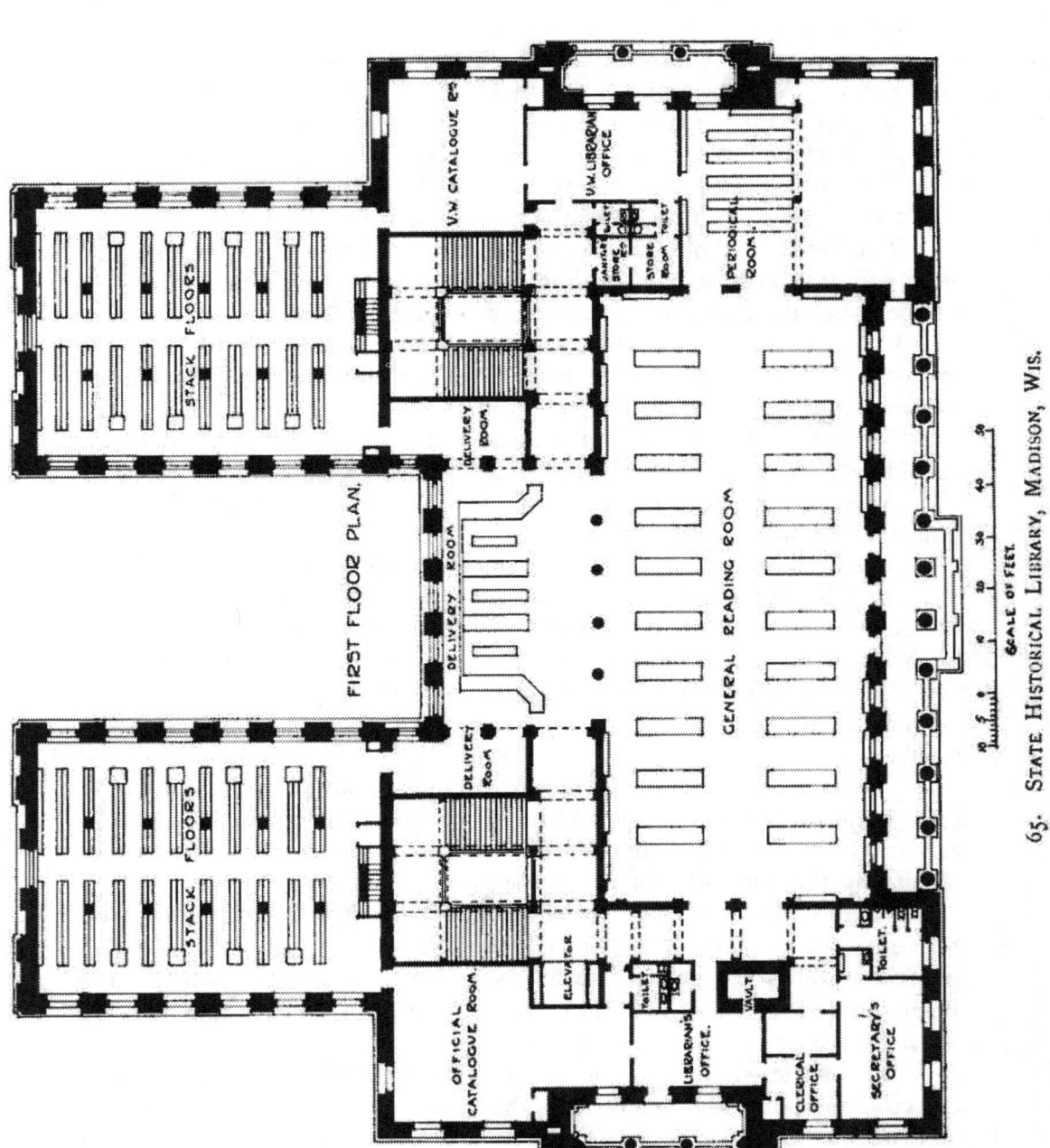

65. State Historical Library, Madison, Wis.

66. Reference Reading Room, Kettering Public Library. *Messrs Goddard & Sons, Architects.*

REFERENCE DEPARTMENT. 95

not only near the entrance but so arranged as to allow of the most direct possible access to any part of the reading room (Fig. 65).

For very special work, small studies of various sizes are sometimes provided as near as possible to the book room (see Figs. 68 and 70, pp. 100 and 125). These must, of course, be well lighted, and may be anything in area from 100 sq. ft. upwards. There is no necessity in this case for any counter, since, the work being of a very special nature, books can be carried to the rooms by the attendants. Small tables and a few chairs are all the furniture required.

67. REFERENCE LIBRARY, KINGSTON PUBLIC LIBRARY.

Alfred Cox, A.R.I.B.A., *Architect*.

Open-Shelf Reference Libraries.—Open-shelf reference libraries may, in the same way as barrier libraries, be divided into two classes, according as the reference books are stored separately or, as is most usual, in the reading room itself.

Where the reference stock is very small, it may be stored in wall-cases round the reading room (Fig. 66), and sometimes the shelving is carried to a considerable height, the upper shelves being approached by galleries or ladders (Fig. 67). The objections to ladders and galleries for public use have been sufficiently demonstrated above, and, where a reference room is arranged on this principle, the upper part of the cases should be used only for bound magazines and volumes seldom in request, while the ladders should not be allowed to be used except by the staff. Even with this restriction, however, the arrangement has the disadvantage of exposing the books in the upper shelves to serious injury from the impure and heated air which always collects near the ceiling unless an unusually efficient system of ventilation is secured.

A far better system is to arrange parallel floor-cases in part of the room, leaving the remainder for reading tables or desks.

Sometimes these floor-cases are arranged to form alcoves for readers, a system which has many æsthetic recommendations and a certain historical interest. Its disadvantages, however, are: in the first place, wastefulness of space; since, to allow of a double-sided table, chairs, and passage room to the shelves, the alcove can hardly be less than about 12 ft. inside the shelving, and should be more to secure freedom from disturbance for those reading in them: in the second, the impossibility of supervision.

On the whole, then, the system previously suggested is to be preferred, though in large libraries it is always an advantage if a reader can obtain a seat near the particular class with which he is working, while the accommodation for those consulting quick-reference books and for readers of magazines also, if such are included, should be kept as far as possible distinct. At the same time, it is generally desirable in arranging the tables to secure the most direct possible access from any seat to any part of the shelving; and whether double or single tables or desks are used, these should be so arranged that the gangways run in the same direction as the bookcases.

As in barrier reference libraries, accommodation must be provided for catalogues, unless there is a separate room for these, and there will also probably be directory-stands, and separate shelves for quick-reference books. In almost every case, except, of course, where the counter of the lending department is in sufficiently close proximity (see Fig. 67), a desk is provided for an attendant; while it is most usual, as a safeguard, to make readers sign their names on entering the room, and therefore a desk or counter accommodation for a ledger is necessary. Sometimes, as in the illustration, readers are admitted to the reference library by means of a wicket and treadle latch worked in the staff enclosure of the lending department.* The catalogues should

---

* For Plan, see Fig. 72, p. 127.

be near to the bookcases as well as to the entrance, a consideration which would suggest as the most satisfactory arrangement one in which the entrance, with the fittings just mentioned, should come in a position intermediate between the reading tables and the bookcases.

In American libraries, in which, as has been said, the whole stock is usually stored together, space is sometimes left in the general book room for the reference readers or for special students (*cf.* Fig. 69), and where there is accurate shelf classification so that a reader can be among all the books on his subject, this system is strongly to be recommended.

Another system is one which allows reference readers to take books from the book room to a reading room opening out of it. This has been done in the United Kingdom in connection with the open-shelf lending library, though how far the confusion of reference readers with borrowers will recommend itself to the generality of librarians is doubtful.

Probably, more especially where reference readers have to sign their names before using the books, many librarians would be willing to allow them to have access to the lending stock upon presenting at the staff enclosure of the lending library a form signed by the attendant in the reference room; though it is again a matter of speculation whether the average library committee would sanction such an arrangement.

Rooms for Special Subjects and Collections.—Occasionally separate rooms are provided for special collections, which may be either books on special subjects or donations given on the condition that they are kept intact.

The system of separating certain classes, and providing, for example, special rooms for fiction and for history, is not generally approved in this country, and would certainly not often be possible or desirable in municipal public libraries. Special collections or donations, however, when of sufficient size, are frequently accommodated in separate rooms.

These rooms, except that they are on a smaller scale, differ in no way as regards their requirements from other reference rooms; though usually the proportion of book accommodation to reading space is smaller than in the latter, and very frequently such collections can be stored entirely in wall-cases.

It is, of course, advisable where possible, for the sake of economy, that such rooms should, when the shelves are open, be supervised by the attendants employed in either the reference or the lending department.

Sometimes, if the collection is artistic or scientific, space has to be provided for the display of works of art or specimens.*

Conclusion.—The small studies sometimes provided for very special work have already been mentioned, and are often found very useful, as is the provision of students' tables in large book rooms.†

With regard, however, to students' reading rooms generally, their presence might often be regarded as a confession of the shortcomings of the reference reading room.

Provided that this is adapted to its purpose, that is to say, if it is so arranged as to ensure favourable conditions and encourage studious reading, there can be no reasonable excuse for establishing what is entirely foreign to the whole spirit of a public library, namely a privileged class.

Very frequently the reference reading room is, as has been said, also a magazine room, and although the presence of a few of the superior magazines may be useful, yet an influx of ordinary magazine readers cannot but destroy the studious character of the room, and therefore such a combination, except within strict limits, is to be avoided.

The provision of a students' reading room in a very large library devoted chiefly or exclusively to reference work is less objectionable; but in most cases the provision of a few small studies or tables in the book rooms would meet all the real requirements in this direction, and make invidious distinctions less conspicuous.

---

* See also under "Spare Rooms," pp. 101 and 102.
† *Cf.* Figs. 68, 69, and 70.

CHAPTER X.

OTHER PUBLIC ROOMS AND SPACES.

General.—In addition to the departments dealt with in the foregoing chapters there remain to be discussed, in the first place, such further items of public accommodation as are not indispensable to the working of a library, yet may be held to enhance its utility: in the second, such necessary parts as entrances, vestibules, and staircases, all of which will be considered in the present chapter.

Public Catalogue Rooms.—In the preceding chapters the accommodation of catalogues has been touched upon, and the use of special rooms for their accommodation has already been mentioned. The position and requirements of such special rooms depend upon the arrangement of the library generally and upon the form of catalogue to be accommodated. A catalogue room for the accommodation of card catalogues should provide space first for the cabinets themselves, secondly for tables and chairs at which readers may consult the cards after removing the drawer they require. When sheaf catalogues are used, the walls will, of course, be fitted with pigeon-holes, and tables and chairs will be necessary in this case also.

In American libraries the catalogues for the whole stock are usually kept in the delivery room, or sometimes in a special room opening out of this, and easily accessible to reference readers (Fig. 69 p. 100).

It is, of course, a great advantage if one catalogue room and one catalogue can be made to suffice both for reference readers and borrowers. It would, however, be hardly possible, where open shelves are adopted, to provide a common catalogue room for the whole library which should be open to borrowers and reference readers. A suggested plan for meeting this difficulty is to provide a double catalogue room with an entrance from the lending library on one side and the reference room on the other, the readers in the one department being separated from the borrowers in the other by a row of cabinets

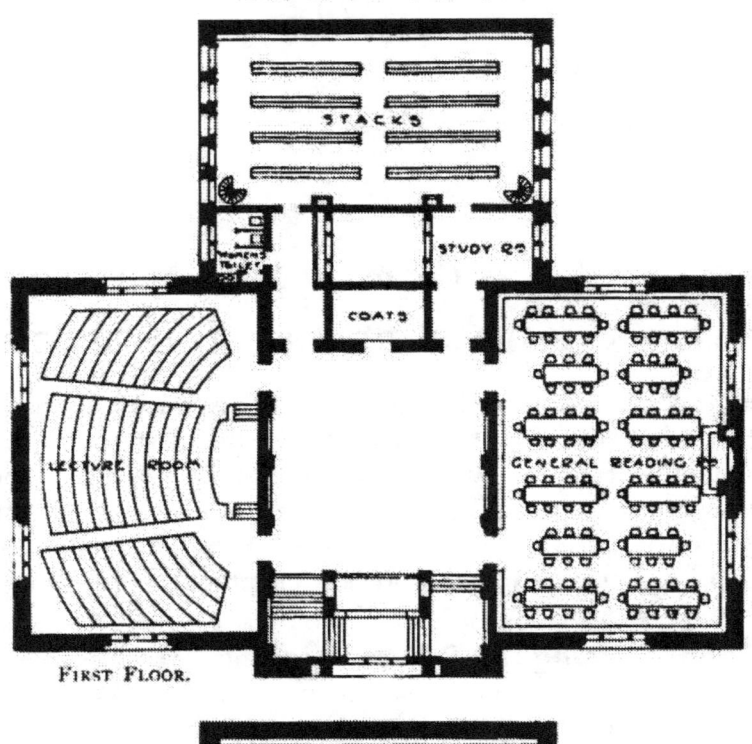

First Floor.

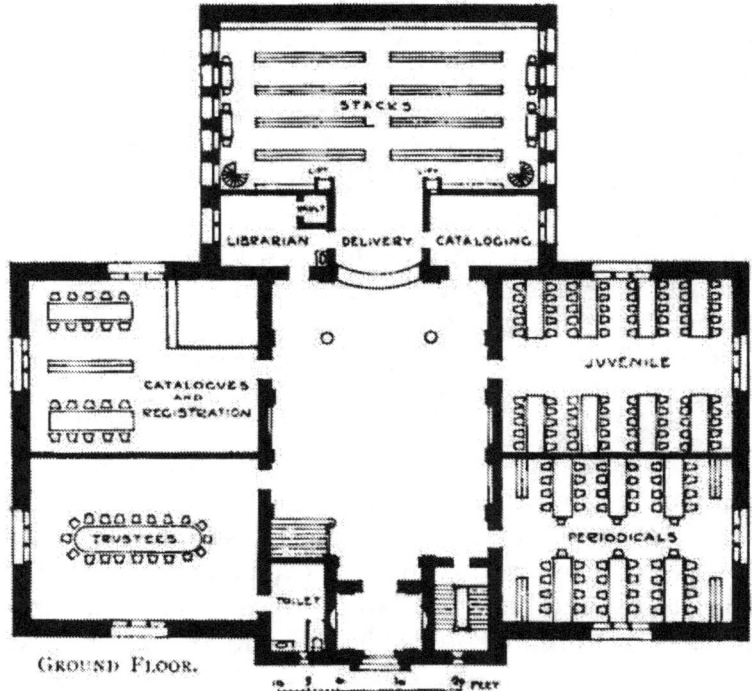

Ground Floor.

68 and 69. Ryerson Public Library, Grand Rapids, Mich.

Shepley, Rutan, & Coolidge, Architects.

or pigeon-holes, according to which form may be in use. If card cabinets were used the drawers would be so made as to pull out in either direction, while the space above would either be left open or glazed so that a person on one side wishing to consult a particular drawer would be able to see if any one on the other side was just going to take hold of it.

If pigeon-holes for sheaf catalogues were used it would, of course, be necessary for each to have the letters contained in the particular sheaf clearly printed on the woodwork.

Lecture Rooms.—The provision of lecture rooms in connection with public libraries cannot but greatly enhance their educational efficiency, and among progressive librarians they are already considered essential.

These rooms in public libraries are used mostly at night, and they are often, therefore, placed in a basement (*cf.* Fig. 81, p. 134). This should, however, only be done when their windows can be at some distance from the nearest roadway. Otherwise the noise is a great drawback.

It is well to provide a platform and to leave a large area of smooth, dead-white wall at this end of the room for magic-lantern pictures, and it is also wise to consider the position of the lantern when arranging the electric wiring, and to provide plugs with which the arc-light of the lantern may be conveniently connected. A special gallery for the lantern is often provided about half-way up the wall opposite the screen. An excellent plan is to place the lantern in a separate room on a balcony or shelf. This has the advantages, especially where cinematograph exhibitions are given, of giving complete isolation in case of fire, and allowing the operator to work in full light.

A method of signalling should be arranged in connection with a lecture room lantern; and it is very desirable, if scientific lectures are given, to have gas, electric current, and water carried to the platform.

It is not generally necessary to provide stepped floors in these rooms.

Spare Rooms.—There are many other details of public accommodation which are to be found in existing public libraries, such as smoking rooms, conversation rooms, museums, and art galleries; though as a general rule it may be said that any unnecessary multiplication of parts tends to increase the difficulties of supervising and working the library.

Smoking rooms would certainly be a blessing to those whom a long stay in a library deprives of their wonted stimulus to thought, but whether their introduction is to be altogether recommended is a question for librarians to answer, and it is usually answered in the negative.

Conversation rooms may certainly be introduced in large libraries, and their presence has the advantage of being a continual reminder of the fact that conversation is not permitted in the reading rooms. In small libraries, however, their advantages cannot be considered equivalent to the loss of space and income involved in their provision. Such libraries should be arranged exclusively with a view to the efficient performance of the proper work of the library, and of this conversation is no essential part.

On the other hand, the addition of a large room, which can be used for committee meetings, lectures, exhibitions, and a variety of other purposes, cannot but be recommended.

Likewise the provision of museums and art galleries in connection with the library is conducive of excellent results, the latter the more especially if in conjunction with a collection of books on art.

Such rooms must, of course, be designed with a view to the particular purposes for which they are intended, and cannot be considered to come within the scope of the present work. If they are likely to be used for concerts while the library is open they should be kept as far from the reading rooms as possible, and certainly not over them. Sound-proof walls and floors should be provided; while it is often advisable to provide separate entrances from the street.

Public Lavatories and Closets.—The provision of public lavatories and closets within library buildings is an example of the way the limited library rate is sometimes sacrificed to extraneous needs.

It does not rightly devolve upon the library to provide a public convenience, which is what a lavatory in a public library often becomes until it is found to be such a nuisance that it has to be closed.

Certainly, in connection with reference reading rooms, it would seem right that at any rate lavatory accommodation should be provided if only to encourage readers to wash before handling the books, and also, if no public lavatory accommodation is provided by the authorities near the library, every facility for a long day's work without interruption should be provided for students, but it is the duty of the municipal authorities rather than the library to see to this. To meet the needs of the public in cases where lecture and other rooms are used for social and other purposes, it may be desirable to provide lavatories and other facilities, but these should only be accessible on such occasions (*cf.* Fig. 77). Where closets are provided, they should always be placed against an outer wall and should not open directly from a room. Indeed it would probably be better to give up all idea of keeping such accommodation for the use of readers only, and make the entrance altogether outside the library. As a rule, however, they had far better be altogether avoided, except under the above-mentioned limitations.

Refreshment Rooms.—For the same reasons as have been given in favour of public lavatories, refreshment rooms might with advantage be provided, if worked on a judicious system, in large libraries; and the basement or an upper floor should be used rather than the ground floor, as accessibility is not of prime importance in this case.

Bicycle Sheds.—The area from which a library is available is, of course, very greatly widened if facilities are afforded for readers to come from a distance on bicycles.

The great difficulty is that no accommodation is usually provided, and this leads to such readers bringing their machines into the corridors and damaging and soiling walls and floors.

The objection to providing bicycle sheds is the responsibility in case of damage to machines left there. It has been suggested that this difficulty should be met by putting notices in the sheds, forbidding their use for bicycles! It would seem, however, that such a cause is one in which library committees ought to be willing to assume a certain amount of responsibility, and even provide some supervision if necessary.

With regard to the accommodation required, that must, of course, be very much a matter of guess work, and as with the building of such sheds the number of bicycles brought would probably increase, the authorities need not feel bound to provide more than a certain limited amount of accommodation.

Public Entrances and Vestibules.—Public entrances need careful supervision, and it is therefore generally advisable that there should be one main entrance. The same applies to exits, though it is best, especially in buildings which accommodate a large number of readers, to provide several emergency exits.

The arrangement of doors in the public entrances of libraries has already been mentioned, but in this connection there is one important item which must not be omitted, namely, the accommodation of advertisement readers. That public libraries should lend themselves to the assistance of those who want work is an attitude with which no one can reasonably find fault; and where newspapers are displayed in the reading room, this room would, in many neighbourhoods, be freely used for the purpose of advertisement reading were not other accommodation provided. Moreover, it is important in the case of employment advertisements that these should be displayed early in the day, often before the library is open.

In some cases the sheets are posted on a hooded board within the grounds of the library, or at some convenient spot near it; and one of these two methods is no doubt best when possible. Often, however, there are neither grounds nor a convenient situation in the neighbourhood, and in such cases a lobby in the entrance of the library itself must be used.

Slopes may be placed against the walls of an outer porch if such exists, or, if not, within the external doors, but outside the inner swing doors or revolving doors as the case may be. When this method is adopted the inner doors should be of such a nature that they cannot be forced or damaged, and occasionally iron folding doors may be used with advantage, since not only are these impassable but they allow of supervision from within.

The use of the vestibule itself, however, is apt to lead to congestion, and another method is to provide a separate lobby at one side of the entrance with a glazed opening or grille for supervision on the inner side.

The size necessary for this will, of course, depend upon the length and arrangement of the slopes. These, as in newspaper rooms, should be multiples of 4 ft. in length, and generally an 8-ft. run, with 5 or 6 ft. clear space behind the slope, will allow ample space for the display of the advertisement sheets of two morning papers. Whether any additional space is necessary for other papers or duplicates must depend on the requirements of the locality.

Of corridors and entrance halls generally it may be said that, while they should be well lighted and of sufficient size to allow of free traffic and sometimes for the accommodation of showcases or works of art, and while they must not look cramped or mean, they should not be wasteful, and excessive corridors are as surely a sign of bad planning in a library as in any other kind of building. Beyond this their size and shape is so entirely dependent on the arrangement of the building that they cannot be generally discussed apart from it.

OTHER PUBLIC ROOMS AND SPACES.

A spacious and dignified entrance hall often makes a good impression on a person entering a library, and if this can be secured without wastefulness of space and money it is a great advantage; while where it can be made to serve the twofold purposes of delivery room and hall, a satisfactory result is often possible.

A box for a porter is often required. This should be placed in the entrance corridor or hall in such a position that he can see those entering and leaving the library and if possible supervise some of the public rooms.

Sometimes a telephone call box has to be installed, and this is another good reason for having plenty of room in the approaches to a library.

Public Staircases.*—Though the ideal library, at any rate if of small or medium size, would probably be on one floor only and staircases consequently unnecessary, the exigencies of cramped sites often make one or more upper floors inevitable. Where the upper floor or floors are much used, two staircases should be available in case of fire; and these should not, of course, if it can be avoided, be in the centre of the building, while they should be continued right up to the full height. The width depends on the amount of traffic with which they have to cope, and generally they should not be less than 5 ft. wide, and sometimes a width of 8 ft. or even rather more is advisable.

Where there is a very large amount of traffic, double stairs divided by a hand-rail separating those ascending from those descending are sometimes recommended, but as a matter of fact it is very hard to impose such regulations effectually.

Separate staircases for those going up and those going down are sometimes recommended, but the same difficulty applies to these.

The stairs should, of course, be in straight flights without winders, well lighted, and not too steep, say from $5\frac{1}{2}$ in. by 13 in. to $6\frac{1}{2}$ in. by 11 in. Wooden hand-rails should always be provided.

The flights should be for preference from ten to fourteen steps.

Great care must, of course, be taken in fixing the positions of staircases, which should not open into narrow corridors where they might cause congestion, nor close to the doors of public rooms.

---

* For general remarks on staircases see Chapter II., pp. 8 and 9.

Chapter XI.

ADMINISTRATIVE ACCOMMODATION.

The size of a library staff depends upon the work and income of the library, and consequently the accommodation needed for it will vary, from one room in a very small library to a considerable number in a large one.

It is intended, in the first place, to point out the chief requirements of different items of staff accommodation; and the question of the amount of accommodation required in libraries of various sizes will be discussed subsequently.*

Consequently the present chapter will deal first with those rooms used for work in connection with the proper business of the library, such as binding, repairing, and cataloguing: next, those required for the management of the institution by the librarian and committee. After that such accommodation will be discussed as is provided for the staff while on the premises and for resident librarians or caretakers; then the provision necessary for heating and cleaning; and lastly such necessary parts as entrances, stairs, and lavatories.

Workrooms.—General workrooms are necessary in all but very small libraries. Their uses are many and various, comprising the preparation of books for issue, general repairs, labelling, cutting, and so on.

A good light is very desirable and the room should usually contain one or two long trestle tables, say 9 to 12 ft. or even more in length, cupboards, drawers for tools and nails, and a few strong chairs or benches, besides shelves.

A stove of some sort is also necessary for boiling paste.

The space required must, of course, depend very much on the work of the library, but a roomy, light, and habitable workroom is an immense help towards the efficient discharge of their duties by the staff.

It is most important that there should be no dark corners in the

---

* Chapter XIV.

ADMINISTRATIVE ACCOMMODATION.

staff rooms, and glazed panels in the doors and fanlights over them may often be introduced with advantage.

Except in very large libraries the workrooms often constitute practically the only accommodation for the staff, and in such cases require in addition to the above many of the fittings prescribed below under the heading of mess-rooms.*

Cataloguing Rooms.—Special rooms for cataloguing are only required in large libraries. Where they are necessary their chief requirements are long tables with a good light on them, a few chairs, shelving, drawers, and so on. They should be near the book rooms.†

Binderies.—Except in very large institutions the books are not usually bound on the premises.

Where, however, this is done a special room is required. This should be as far removed from the reading rooms as possible, since the work carried on in it entails considerable noise, and the process of finishing and lettering in gold-leaf produces a very unpleasant smell.

The best plan is to place the bindery at the top of the building, since a good light is very necessary, and it is an advantage if this comes from above. The ventilation, owing to the smell, should be very thorough.

With regard to fittings and furniture, the requirements usually include a binding press, workman's bench, tool-boxes and racks, cupboards for leather, and a locker for gold-leaf and valuable books, pegs for coats, and shelves for books waiting to be bound; a gas stove for heating the tools used for numbering and lettering is also necessary, as is a stove or grate for drying. Water must also be provided in this room.

Receiving and Packing Rooms.—A separate room for receiving cases of new books, and for packing those which are to be sent away to be bound, is extremely useful in a library of any size, as these processes cause a considerable mess and litter.

They should be as near as possible to an entrance, for preference one not used by the public.

These rooms should, of course, be either on or below the entrance level and not above it.

If they are in a basement, a shoot from the outside for heavy

---

* Page 110. † See Fig. 69.

packing-cases is very useful, while a lift to the main floor is desirable in large libraries (*cf.* Fig. 71, p. 125).

Store-Rooms.—Store-rooms for stationery and all sorts of materials and odds and ends should be provided in large libraries. These should, of course, be near the workrooms. Usually, however, cupboards or shelves in the rooms already dealt with will suffice for such purposes.

Librarian's Room.—The librarian's room is a very important item of accommodation as regards not only its position, but also its requirements.

In respect of the former, it is a very frequent mistake to consider the librarian as a sort of policeman, and to give him an office surrounded by glass screens where he is supposed apparently to spend his time watching every part of the building.

Such an arrangement shows, of course, an absolute ignorance of the duties and responsibilities of a librarian.

These, as it should be hardly necessary to say, are such as to give him ample employment apart from all question of supervision. The whole administrative and economic organisation of the institution is practically in his hands, and it is through his staff rather than directly that he must keep in touch with the public.

Consequently the room in which his work is performed must not be in the way of every disturbance, but in a quiet part of the building; and it should communicate with the working spaces for the staff rather than directly with the public rooms or vestibules.

In large libraries an outer office for the public is sometimes provided, and from this there should be a second exit, as a way of escape from importunate callers, canvassers, and other administrative nuisances.

Of course, in very small libraries the duties of librarian and staff are usually concentrated in one person, and in such cases the librarian must exercise all the necessary supervision. During most of the time, he, or she, as the case may be, will be engaged most probably in the lending library, and the proper duties of librarianship, which in this case will not, it is to be supposed, be extensive, must be attended to when the library is unfrequented or at times when the building, or at any rate the lending department, is closed. Even then it is doubtful whether a separate room in a quiet part is not, with intermittent supervision only, to be preferred to the sort of conservatory so often provided.

The requirements of the room itself are that it should be, as has been said, quiet, well lighted, and sufficiently spacious to take, conveniently and without overcrowding, all the necessary fittings and furniture.

With regard to these, every librarian's room should be provided with a sufficient amount of shelving, though as a rule wall-cases on two or at most three sides will be ample; while a revolving bookcase on which he can place books in immediate use near his desk is always useful. A nest of drawers from 3 to 4 ft. high along one side or part of a side of the room is also very desirable. A large table, say 7 ft. by 5 ft., is also very useful for accommodating books, papers, and circulars until they can be attended to and disposed of.

If the room is also used for committee meetings a considerably larger table may be necessary.

At any rate one other small table is desirable for typewriting and other purposes, and a third table for a letter-press may with advantage be included.

An office chair and a good roll-top or pedestal desk with lock-up drawers and pigeon-holes for correspondence are among quite the most essential items of the equipment of this room. In addition to this the librarian should have a small safe for cash in his room, while, since he often has to receive visitors and occasionally deputations, the room should be provided with five or six ordinary chairs, and there should, of course, be a waste-paper basket.

Usually a librarian prefers to have an open fire in his room, and in this case a good mantel-shelf should be provided, as every place on which odds and ends can be placed is valuable in a room which is usually overcrowded with a very heterogeneous litter.

A private lavatory and closet should usually be provided for the librarian.

Committee Rooms.—Library committees vary in size from seven or eight members to thirty and over. With very small committees the librarian's room is usually of sufficient size for their meetings, while often, when they are large, some room in the municipal offices can be used. It is, however, a good thing, even where this is done, to provide a spare room which may be used by the committee. This room should be close to the librarian's room, and, if possible, connected with it by a door.

The chief requirement of a committee room is that it should provide space for a table sufficiently large to accommodate the number of which the committee consists; but it should also be well lighted and comfortable, though not too high, since the acoustic properties of very high rooms are often not good. In some libraries lockers are provided for the use of committee-men, as well as umbrella stands, hat racks, and other fittings. This room is, as a rule, the only one in a library which glories in the luxury of a Turkey or other rich carpet.

Strong-Rooms.—A strong-room for registers, minutes, and records, and occasionally for rare books, should be provided in every library of any size. This room must be well ventilated and thoroughly fireproof, and should be accessible from the librarian's room and committee room.

It should be provided with shelving round the walls, and space should be left for a table in the centre.

Cupboards for stationery may also be provided with advantage. The size will, of course, vary according to the requirements, and may be anything from 4 ft. by 6 ft. to 2 ft. by 20 ft. The lighting, though it may be artificial only, must be good.

If electric light is used, the switch should generally be outside.

Mess-Rooms.—As has been said above, the workrooms, except in libraries of considerable size, are usually the only rooms which can serve as sitting rooms for the staff.

In large libraries, however, mess-rooms are often provided, and where there are both male and female attendants separate rooms are desirable. The size of these rooms must, of course, depend upon the number of the staff. Generally speaking, they should be bright, cheerful rooms, fitted with separate lockers, one for each member of the staff, hat and coat pegs, unless these are provided elsewhere, one or more tables, and chairs; while a stove at which food can be cooked is necessary. At least one small looking-glass is also desirable in female mess-rooms. The walls should be fitted with picture rails, as the room should be made as attractive as possible.

Librarian's and Caretaker's Residences.—In many libraries a residence for the librarian is provided in the building. This is usually wholly or partially on one of the upper floors, though a situation over much frequented public rooms cannot be recommended from a hygienic point of view.

ADMINISTRATIVE ACCOMMODATION.

The provision of a residence has not, however, been found to effect the economy intended, since the librarian is usually unwilling to pay more for a superior house than he would have to pay for one which would fulfil his actual requirements. Consequently the saving in salary does not repay the extra cost in building.

Where therefore the architect has to include accommodation for a librarian he should avoid making this unnecessarily commodious, and should not provide more than five or at most six rooms in addition to bathroom, closet, and the necessary offices.

A separate entrance and staircase should be provided, and direct communication with the library is an advantage, though this has sometimes to be dispensed with where the rating authority makes it an excuse for assessing the whole building as a habitable house.

When the kitchen is on an upper floor, a conveniently placed lift should be provided in order to obviate the necessity of tradesmen taking their goods up the stairs.

A somewhat better arrangement, if it is deemed inadvisable that the library should not be left unguarded at night, is to provide accommodation for a resident caretaker either in the attics or preferably, for reasons indicated above, in a basement. The accommodation necessary would be one fair-sized kitchen and living-room of about 150 sq. ft., scullery, closet, coal cellar, one fair-sized bedroom, and one or, for preference, two small ones (see Fig. 79).

It is, of course, an inconvenient and generally unworkable arrangement to have both the librarian and a caretaker in the same building.

Heating Chamber and Fuel Stores.—The position, dimensions, and other requirements of the heating chamber and fuel store will, of course, depend upon the system of heating employed, and also upon the size of the library.

Most usually this department requires to be in a basement or half-basement in order that the boiler may be below the level of the radiators.

Sometimes, in order to avoid the risk of fire, the heating department is separated from the main block (see Fig. 71), but when other precautions are taken this would seem to involve an unnecessary additional cost. It is, however, a good thing that the entrance should be so arranged that dust and dirt from the heating chamber cannot enter the library.

For this reason it is best, where possible, to provide an entirely separate entrance from the outside to the heating chamber, though this, of course, is not generally in one of the main fronts of the building.

The dimensions must, as has been said, vary according to the system used and the size of the apparatus to be accommodated, that is to say, there must be room in the heating chamber itself for the accommodation of the requisite boilers or other appliances, and sufficient space for stoking, cleaning, and so on; while the fuel store must give sufficient space for the storage of coal and coke in such quantities as will suffice for a considerable time and not necessitate frequent replenishment.

Often a great deal of time is wasted by reason of a badly planned fuel store, and the arrangement of this should be very carefully considered. In the first place, it is most important, more especially where the fuel is delivered in cart-loads or truck-loads rather than in sacks, that carts should be able to drive right up to the shoot or whatever form of opening is provided. The opening also should be so placed in relation to the store that the latter may be filled as nearly as possible to the limit of its capacity without it being necessary for a man to stand by and shovel it along as it is shot in.

For this reason it is best in an oblong fuel store that the shoot should be as near as possible to the centre of one of the longer sides, unless the size requires more than one shoot, when they should be well distributed; while in order to facilitate the removal of the fuel to the furnaces the opening or openings between the fuel store and the heating chamber should occupy corresponding positions in the opposite side. It is sometimes necessary, when the heating apparatus is on a scale to demand more or less continuous attention, to provide a closet in connection with it for the man in charge.

Cleaners' Sinks and Cupboards.—Sinks with draw-taps for the use of cleaners, and cupboards for their apparatus, should be provided in convenient places, and in large libraries there should be at least one sink on each floor.

The cupboards should, of course, be provided with locks, and the sinks should not be accessible to the public.

Waste-Paper Bins.—Fireproof bins should be provided in large libraries for waste-paper in such positions that the contents can be easily removed from the building.

Entrances, Staircases, and Lavatories.—Except in very

small libraries it is usually an advantage to provide a separate entrance for librarian and staff by which they may enter or leave the building at times when the public door is not open. A separate entrance for the delivery of parcels is also most desirable in a large library, while side doors by which books may be taken into the open to be dusted are often useful.

Staircases, also, for the use of the staff only are often necessary. These do not require as great a width as those used by the public, though they should not generally be less than 3 ft. wide, nor is it necessary for the rise to be quite so easy. Spiral staircases and, where books have to be carried up or down, winders, also, should, if possible, be avoided.

The provision of special lavatories and closets for the attendants is, of course, most necessary, and, as with mess-rooms, separate accommodation should be provided for the sexes when both are employed.

Chapter XII.

FINANCE, ORGANISATION, AND BUILDING.

Income and Expenditure.*—The idea that a library building should provide accommodation for an indefinitely increasing stock has already been disposed of, while the desire of erecting at all costs a pretentious edifice will be dealt with below; yet these two causes have often resulted in such an impoverishment of a library that the proper equipment and maintenance of the fabric and its contents have been impossible, with the result that the educational utility of the institution has been reduced to a minimum, if not entirely annulled.

For a library to attain its maximum of efficiency it is essential that its aims should be subordinated to its financial conditions; in other words, the cost of site, building, and furniture must be such as to leave an ample proportion of the income to cover the working expenses of the institution.

The library rate, usually one penny in the pound, is, as has been said, the main source of income, though there are other variable and often unreliable sources from which funds are derived, such as donations, grants, the sale of securities, fines, and so on. The expenditure, in addition to those items connected with the cost of building and furnishing—that is to say, the repayments of interest and principal on loans—includes repairs and maintenance, the supply of literature, salaries of staff, and so on.

Some idea of the various items of expenditure, and a judicious distribution of them in libraries with various incomes, may be gathered from the following hypothetical budgets.†

---

* The financial questions connected with municipal public libraries are very manifold, and in the present work no attempt is made to deal with the subject exhaustively. For such a treatment the reader is referred to J. D. Brown's "Library Economy," to which the writer is indebted for a large part of the matter of the present chapter, and to which the reader will be frequently referred in the following pages.

† From J. D. Brown's "Manual of Library Economy," § 53, *q.v.*

FINANCE, ORGANISATION, AND BUILDING.

Items of Expenditure.	Income from Rate.						
	£3,000.	£2,500.	£2,000.	£1,500.	£1,000.	£500.	£100.
	£	£	£	£	£	£	£ s.
Buildings—							
Lighting	180	150	110	75	50	30	6 0
Heating	30	25	20	10	8	5	2 0
Water	10	8	6	3	2	1	
Fittings and Repairs	40	30	22	20	10	5	} 3 0
Cleaning and Materials	30	25	18	15	8	4	
Rent	—	—	—	—	—	70	25 0
Insurance	12	10	8	6	5	3	0 5
Books, &c.—							
Books, Maps, Prints	500	400	300	200	100	50	10 0
Periodicals and Newspapers	180	150	110	80	50	40	10 0
Bookbinding	110	90	70	50	30	15	2 0
Salaries—							
Librarian	350	325	300	250	200	150	30 0
Sub-Librarian	175	163	150	125	100	—	—
Senior Assistants	(1) 78	(1) 60	(1) 60	60	—	—	—
Junior Assistants (£26 each)	(8) 208	(6) 160	(5) 130	(3) 78	(3) 78	(2) 52	—
Caretakers (20s., 25s., 30s. each)	(2) 130	(2) 130	(1) 78	65	65	52	—
Cleaners (5s. weekly each)	(4) 60	(3) 39	(3) 39	(2) 26	13	—	10 0
Establishment Charges—							
Stationery	30	20	12	10	8	5	
Printing	50	30	20	15	8	5	
Local Rates	15	12	8	6	—	—	
Taxes	10	8	7	6	4	2	} 1 15
Carriages and Travelling Expenses	20	10	12	10	5	2	
Postages	12	15	8	5	3	2	
Miscellaneous Supplies	20	15	12	10	3	—	
Loans Account—							
Principal & Interest	750	625	500	375	250	—	—

It will be seen that in this table the expenditure on the loans account is one-quarter of the library's income from the rate, and this should be considered the limit.

Moreover, no account has been taken on the one hand of receipts other than the library rate, nor on the other of any expenditure in connection with loans on sites, the latter being considered as likely to be more than balanced by the former.

When possible, the necessity for a loan on a site should be avoided, and often a public library is presented with a gift of land from some individual or body, and indeed town councils and others are legally empowered to convey sites to the library authority. Every attempt should be made to obtain a site on such terms, or at any rate at a nominal rental, though this, of course, is not always possible.

In the same way, with a view to the reduction or entire removal of the expenditure on a building loan, where possible, donations towards the building, and better still a gift of the whole building, provided it be not disproportionate to the income available for working and maintenance, should be obtained. The effect on the statistics produced by the donations of various well-known supporters of the public library movement has been very considerable, but, as indicated above, it is important that such gifts should not be made under conditions which tend to defeat their own end.

With regard to the periods for which sums may be borrowed, these are fixed by the Local Government Board, and are usually as follows*:—

For sites or lands	60 or 50 years.
For buildings (including fixtures like counters, screens, wall and standard bookcases, wall newspaper slopes, barriers, &c.)	30 years.†
For books	10 years.
For furniture (tables, chairs, desks, and movable furniture only)	10 years.

It is important that all fixtures should be included in the building loan in order to secure the longer time for repayment.

The rate of interest, of course, varies from time to time, $3\frac{1}{2}$ per cent. to $3\frac{3}{4}$ per cent. being a fair average.

The maximum of expenditure, then, on loans for buildings and furniture may be taken as one-fourth of the income of the library, and it is important in this connection to consider the proportion which the cost of the latter—that is, movable furniture—should bear to that of the former. Very often a quite insufficient amount is left for furnishing, and the consequence is that cheap and shoddy stuff has to be used. As

---

* "Library Economy," James Duff Brown, 1903. § 37, p. 26.

† A loan for purchasing an existing building will not be sanctioned by the Local Government Board for a term exceeding twenty or twenty-five years.

a general rule, it may be taken that 10 per cent. at least of the whole cost should be set aside for this purpose.

For instance, if a library has an income of £1,000 from the rate, the amount it can afford to pay annually on buildings and furniture will be £250, which will represent a loan for the former of, say, about £3,600, for the latter of about £400.

When the income is very small, that is to say, anything much below £1,000, it is, of course, impossible for the library to erect a new building except by the help of donations; and where these are not forthcoming or sufficient, premises must be rented for the purpose.

The figures given above are, of course, hypothetical, and must be considered as approximations only. They are subject to considerable modifications in particular circumstances, most especially, of course, when buildings are presented.

Sites and Distribution.—The selection of a site for a public library is a very important matter, as a bad situation is one of the greatest drawbacks to efficiency.

The requirements of the site are twofold. On the one hand, it must provide sufficient and suitable space for the building required to be erected immediately, while leaving room for any probable future additions: on the other, it should be so situated with regard to its surroundings that, while no external cause shall interfere with the satisfactory use of the library for those purposes for which it is intended, it may be accessible to the greatest possible number of those for whose benefit it is erected.

With regard to the former of these requirements, it is obvious that a site so cramped by boundaries, party-walls, building lines, ancient lights, and other restrictions that it will with difficulty contain the building to be immediately erected, not only makes straightforward and satisfactory planning difficult or impossible, but allows no possibility of future expansion. Even if the prospect of extension has to be given up altogether, it is important that the site should not only provide ample space, but should be conveniently shaped, with a view to the internal arrangements, aspect of rooms, and so on. A very good library might be planned on a piece of land 100 ft. by 100 ft., or 10,000 sq. ft., while a site of the same area, but measuring 40 ft. by 250 ft., could not but involve many inconvenient arrangements and much waste of space. Moreover, steep gradients, though the difficulties they offer may sometimes be overcome by ingenious planning, do not tend either to convenience or economy. Lastly, a dry soil and one affording a good foundation is most essential.

Consequently it is necessary that the site should be ample in area, and of convenient dimensions: the ground level, dry, and firm.

With regard to the position of the site in relation to its neighbourhood, it is, of course, most important that while it must be near to as many as possible of the library's potential patrons, it should not be exposed to risks of fire, to dust, noise, and impediments to light.

All of these disadvantages are most noticeable where the library has to be erected immediately on a busy street, and therefore such a situation should be avoided where a suitable and sufficiently accessible site can be obtained elsewhere.

At the same time, the building should not be so placed that it is not seen. The visibility of a library building is its best advertisement, and therefore a great factor in its scope and utility.

Frequently accessible and sufficiently central sites can be obtained where the library can be set well back from the nearest road, and where open space is secured on either side, being either part of the library plot, or such permanent open spaces as public parks, recreation grounds, or disused cemeteries.

Where the library must perforce be on a street this should be a fairly quiet one, rather than a bustling thoroughfare, though the neighbourhood of such is a guarantee of the accessibility of the library.

In consideration of the risk of fire, it is important that the library should be as far as possible isolated from other buildings, and the neighbourhood of shops especially should be avoided.

Isolated sites are too, of course, preferable as affording better facilities for lighting; while in order to ensure freedom from dust and noise, busy and narrow streets must be avoided, and the building set back as far as possible.

The difficulties of securing sufficient light, especially where this is of necessity obtained largely from the street front, are very great in a narrow street with tall houses on the opposite side. An angle of 45 degrees from the sills is usually accepted as the test of the maximum height to which buildings can be carried without interfering with light, but a considerably lesser angle is preferable. Where such obstructions cannot be avoided, prismatic glass should be used.

The question of accessibility, as has been said, is specially important, since a man's inclination to visit a library varies inversely as the difficulty of getting to it, and of course when a library is at some distance, a good deal of time may be spent in going backwards and forwards. Indeed, the existence of locally supported public libraries is entirely due to the recognition of the need for greater accessibility than can be afforded by great national collections, and it is therefore only fitting that, when a library is opened for the benefit of those residing or working within a certain municipality, the building should be so placed as to be as useful as possible to as many as possible.

The determination of the most suitable situation is not always an easy matter, and the position sought should be central, not from a geographical point of view, but from one taking into consideration the life of the municipality and various particular local conditions; for which reason it is impossible to make any definite suggestions which shall apply generally.

This question of accessibility makes itself most felt when the administrative area which the library serves is a wide one, involving considerable distances. In the case, for instance, of a large town with outlying suburbs one library would be practically useless to a large number of the inhabitants.

The solution of the difficulty is the same as in the case of Mahomet and the mountain; in other words, it must be met by the establishment of travelling libraries, delivery stations, or branch libraries. The last is the only form of local distribution which requires special buildings, and is far commoner in this country than either of the other two.

The qualifications of the site for a branch library are similar to those mentioned above. The question of distribution and the relative position of branch to branch and branch to central is always a difficult one, and one which must depend on local circumstances. It is sometimes said that no ratepayer should have to walk more than half a mile to a library or he will not go to it; but such standards are, of course, usually impracticable. Where possible, the libraries should not be more than about a mile from each other, and should, of course, be so arranged as to embrace as much of the administrative area as possible within half-mile radii from each centre. The population cannot usually be taken as a basis, but it has been suggested * that there should be one library to every 40,000 in closely populated, and one to every 25,000 or 30,000 in scattered districts.

Selection and Employment of Architect.—As has been

---

* "Branch Libraries: Their Number and Cost," by C. W. Sutton, M.A. (*Library Association Record*, vol. vi., No. 2.)

already said, it is most important that the librarian, in whose hands the working of the library is to be placed at the most critical stage in its career, should be appointed before anything is done towards obtaining designs. It is a still further advantage if he can be appointed before even the site is fixed upon, and in this matter the advice of an architect also should certainly be sought.

The architect for the building itself is in most cases selected by competition, open to all architects.

The question as to whether this method is the best is one of considerable difficulty.

From the point of view of architects generally, competitions have the advantage of giving openings to those whose abilities would otherwise escape recognition, and from that of the library authority it may be pointed out that by obtaining a number of designs they are perhaps more likely to find one which meets their requirements.

On the other hand, it is almost impossible to make instructions so comprehensive that an architect who does not already understand the requirements of a library building can be taught on the spur of the moment this very special branch of his art; and, if he has a knowledge of the requirements, he not unfrequently finds himself bound by the instructions to adopt ideas which, often rightly, his opinion refuses to endorse. Indeed, such instructions, being, as they almost always are, based on those provided for previous competitions, are at any rate apt to check development and the growth of new ideas; while open competitions are seldom such as to allure architects of established reputation and therefore little leisure.

Undoubtedly it is a great advantage for an architect, especially if he understands the special conditions, to be able to thoroughly discuss matters with the librarian before anything is committed to paper, but, as has been said above, librarians do not, as a rule, understand architecture, nor the majority of architects libraries; and such an arrangement requires qualities on both sides which are not, unfortunately, the invariable concomitants of human nature.

Such a co-operation between librarian and architect is, however, desirable even in the case of competitions.

The assessor should, of course, always be an architect (the power of fully understanding architectural drawings being rare among laymen), and one of established reputation and integrity. It is important, also, that he should have a good knowledge of modern library requirements, a necessity often overlooked, though perhaps the worst of all is a man who thinks he knows all about it and wishes to teach the librarian his business.

The librarian and architectural assessor should together draw up the instructions.

These should be accompanied by a block plan of the site, with levels and all particulars of sewers, water supply, and so on, and should indicate the methods of administration which would be adopted, the number of volumes to be accommodated, the cost of the building and everything special to the particular case; but not maxims applicable to library buildings generally.

The rooms required are usually specified, often the number of seats and the various fittings, and many other particulars. As a general rule, however, it is best to confine the instructions to the special requirements, and to leave as much as possible to the discretion of the competitors.

With regard to the question of cost, it may be pointed out that nothing is gained by the practice—only too frequent in competitions—of demanding accommodation far in excess of the price allowed. The result of this method is only too often apparent in overcrowded reading rooms and cramped lending libraries.

The decision of the architectural assessor should be final.

The question between open and limited competitions is a very important one. Open competitions for library buildings are, as has been said, such that none but those who have plenty of time to spare would think of entering them. The conditions of competition, too, are very frequently such that no architect should accept them. There are two by no means unusual clauses in particular to which architects should object; the first giving the advertisers the right to refuse to employ the winning or any other competitor: the second appropriating all premiated designs, whether executed or not, to the advertising body.

With regard to the first, some palliation of the apparent unreasonableness of it may be recognised in the fact that in an absolutely open competition it is difficult for a committee to bind itself to entrust a responsible task to any one who may have satisfied the assessor on paper. This would, however, seem an argument against open competitions rather than one in favour of an equivocal condition. The second, that is, the detention of all the premiated drawings, appears to have little justification, and to give dangerous opportunities for plagiarism and dishonesty. The absence of a reputable architectural assessor should always be an insurmountable objection, since there is, in such a case, no guarantee for architects of a competent or honest decision.

The system of only supplying conditions and instructions on the deposit of a fee does very little good, except to reduce the number of drawings submitted—a doubtful advantage.

An architect should be allowed to see the instructions before deciding whether he wishes to compete, and it is absurd that if he decides not to do so, he should have to dash off a ridiculous set of drawings in order to get back his deposit; especially as there is always a chance of these being selected and carried out!

On the whole, except perhaps in the provinces where the conflicting interests of local practitioners may lead to endless petty intrigues and machinations, the balance of advantages would appear to lie with the middle course between the selection of an individual and an open competition, that is to say, a competition limited to certain selected architects.

Even in this case quite a small number, not more than ten, and for preference only three or four, should be invited.

They should, of course, be selected on account of their general as well as their special knowledge and experience.

In such a case there is no excuse for any reservation as to the employment of the competitor whose design is placed first, and the decision of the assessor should be absolutely binding upon this point.

When once the architect is selected, he should be invited to make suggestions as to any modifications in the design, as required by the original instructions, and should, of course, be consulted on all points connected with the execution of the work.

Chapter XIII.

PRINCIPLES OF PUBLIC LIBRARY DESIGN.

In designing a public library building the essential requirement is, of course, the provision of such space as shall be adequate for the work which the library has to do. The extent of this will usually depend, as has been said, upon its income. There are, however, certain general principles which apply to all public library buildings as such, and these will be considered before any calculation is attempted as to the relation between the income and the accommodation to be provided in various cases. These principles affect, first, the division of the space into departments according to the various purposes for which the building is to be used, and the disposition of the same; and secondly, the architectural treatment of the fabric.

It has been said[*] that "the interior ought to be planned before the exterior is considered," and, though some fault may be found with the expression, the idea intended is indisputably right. There can be no doubt that the utility of the building, more especially in respect of the purposeful arrangement of the various departments, must take precedence of all æsthetic considerations; though it must be remembered that a scheme that looks well on paper generally works well in the concrete.

The question of arrangement will, therefore, be discussed first, and after that the artistic treatment of the whole both internally and externally.

Disposition of Departments.—The first necessity in connection with the disposition of the various parts of a library is that it shall be adapted to the work of the library according to the methods employed.

That is to say, that while both the human occupants and the contents of the library must be afforded every protection from unsuitable and harmful conditions, the convenience of the public on the one

---

[*] "*Points of Agreement among Librarians as to Library Architecture.*" Charles C. Soule. The Brochure Series of Architectural Education. Nov. 1897. Boston.

hand, in their use of the library, must be studied: on the other, every facility must be given for the easy and efficient performance of their duties by the staff.

To these must be added another consideration, namely, economy in cost, maintenance, and working, which, though an essential element in all branches of architecture, has in this case an added importance due to the financial basis on which the system is founded; while again it is frequently necessary in library planning to consider the possibility of growth in the future.

In regard to the care of books, a good deal has already been said, and many of the questions affecting their disposition will be considered below as being essentially connected with the administrative methods of the library.

Though the welfare of books depends more on the nature of the accommodation provided for them than on its position in relation to the other departments, nevertheless a certain amount may be done in the way of protecting them from the injurious influences to which books are peculiarly liable, such as damp, direct sunlight, dust, foul air, dry heat, and fire, by means of a judicious disposition of the building.

With regard to the first of these, namely damp, it has already been suggested that there should be a basement or, at any rate, an air space below the lowest floor of a book room or stack, and, where the site is moist, every possible precaution should be taken to prevent the damp from rising to where the books are stored.

The question of direct sunlight has already been dealt with, and it is a good thing, if possible, to so arrange a book room that it can be sufficiently lighted from the north exclusively. Often, however, this would involve disproportionate inconveniences in other parts of the building, and in such cases the difficulty must be met by the use of blinds.

There are no possible means by which dust can be absolutely excluded from book rooms, and the only thing that can be done is to keep it as far as possible in check, and to remove what does settle in spite of precautions. A certain amount can be done by so arranging the building that the windows of book rooms do not give immediately on to any road or street, and that no door leading to a book room, if the entrance to the library leads directly from a street, is so placed that dust will be carried through when both are open. The latter consideration is one which may, in some cases, affect the question of leaving the borrowers' space open to the vestibule. Provided, however, that there is a reasonable intervening distance, and that the entrance is adequately screened by inner doors, the additional amount of dust penetrating to the books would probably be inconsiderable.

With regard to injury to books from foul and dry air, this most usually occurs when the shelving is carried up to the top of a room which is much used by the public, or in which coal gas is burned. The remedy for this is, of course, obvious and has been mentioned elsewhere.

It is sometimes said that books should never be stored over any public room, unless the intervening floor is made practically air-tight.

It is always very desirable, where possible, that large book rooms or stacks should be so placed that a through draught can be obtained.

With a view to lessening the risk of fire, in many cases where the stack system is employed, it has been thought advisable to detach the stack-rooms as far as possible from the rest of the building (cf. Fig. 65); and often in such cases complete isolation is secured by means of fire-proof doors and shutters.

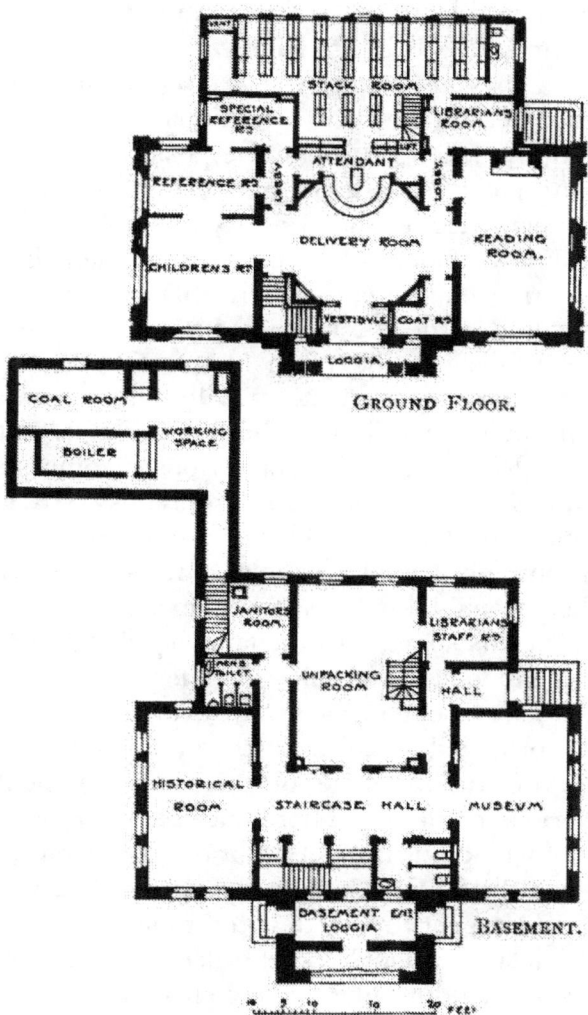

70 AND 71. PLAN FOR CARNEGIE LIBRARY OTTUMWA, IA.

F. R. Comstock, Architect.

As has been said above in connection with fire-prevention, the costliness of the means of assuring complete non-inflammability is so great that it cannot be attempted by municipal public libraries dependent on a very limited rate. This applies as much to the isolation of the books as to the selection of materials and methods of construction; while such isolation is only possible where the stack system is employed.

Librarians' or caretakers' residences and heating chambers are the most likely sources of a conflagration, and if possible they should be so placed as to reduce to a minimum the risk of fire spreading from them to the books* (Figs. 70 and 71).

In considering the arrangement of public rooms, it must be remembered that such conditions as light, quiet, and fresh air are very largely dependent upon the position of the rooms not only in relation to external surroundings, but to one another. In regard to lighting, the aspects recommended above† should, where possible, be secured, while windows should be so placed that their light is not obstructed by neighbouring buildings. Where this cannot be avoided a top-light has to be secured, either by keeping the building wholly or partially on one floor, or by placing the room in question at the top of the building, which latter arrangement has usually the advantage of securing more quiet, and better ventilation, though, perhaps, at the expense of accessibility.

Rooms intended for serious reading should be always separated as far as possible not only from busy streets but from all parts of the building itself in which there is much traffic. A reference reading room, for instance, should always be separated from public passages, borrowers' lobbies, or newspaper reading rooms.

It is sometimes recommended that the greater part of the public accommodation should be under one ceiling divided up by low glazed screens or open arcades, or even that one large undivided room should be provided for all departments in common.

Certainly none of these arrangements can be recommended for serious reading. There may be a few who can read to advantage with the whole business of a library going on within sight and hearing, but such distractions cannot be agreeable to the average reader. Consequently every room devoted to studious work, a reference reading room for instance, should be afforded as much isolation as possible. Borrowers from a lending library, of course, and possibly, too, readers of light periodical literature do not need so much quiet, and the abolition of walls where only these classes are concerned is on occasions defensible for reasons which will be considered and discussed below.

In the same way, no room devoted to serious reading should ever be a passage room, though here again an exception may perhaps be made in the case of newspaper reading rooms or borrowers' lobbies (*cf.*

---

* See page 27. † Pages 10 and 11.

Figs. 79 and 92), where the coming and going is in any case continuous. There must always, however, be considerable inconvenience and disturbance to those sitting in the passage room, if not to those who have to pass through it. The only case in which it can be considered entirely harmless is where the department used as a passage is so spacious as to allow of a wide gangway, and the room approached through it not frequented to any very great extent : the latter requirement being too often, unfortunately, apparent in the case of the reference reading room.

The question of the accessibility of the public rooms is a very important one. Not only should the traffic in the rooms themselves be unhindered by such obstructions as piers and columns, but the approach to them from the entrance and from other departments should be as direct and easy as possible, so as to cause a minimum of delay and confusion.

It has already been pointed out how the full advantages which a library offers often remain unknown unless they are literally thrust upon the public. For this reason the existence of each department of public accommodation should be made amply evident to a stranger entering the building, since people are usually reluctant of exploring unfamiliar corridors.

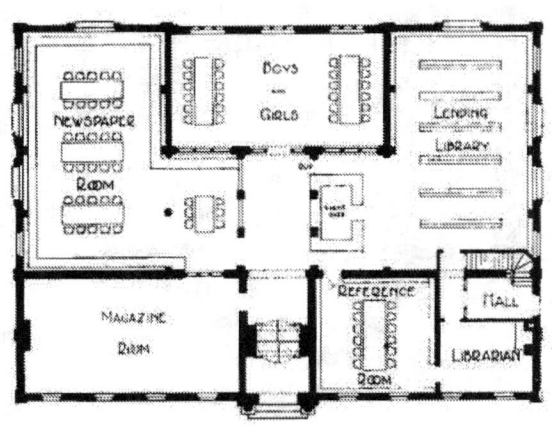

72. KINGSTON PUBLIC LIBRARY.
Alfred Cox, F.R.I.B.A., *Architect*.

Boldly printed notices and finger-boards are, of course, very useful, but the ideal arrangement is one which enables a person entering the library to see before him the door of each public room.

Such a consideration is in favour of a compact central vestibule as opposed to long corridors, such as is often to be found in American libraries and in not a few of those in this country (Figs. 72 and 73).

A further step in this direction would be to adopt a more or less uniform plan for library buildings, a method which, though often impossible owing to the difficulty of obtaining suitable sites, has nevertheless been put into practice in the case of a system of branch libraries. By this means a reader familiar with one branch will be at home on entering any other on the same system, and if such uniformity can be obtained with the compact planning recommended above the result is very near perfection.

Such a compact grouping of the departments implies, of course, that all the rooms should be on the ground floor level, a condition which, owing to the difficulty and cost of securing suitable sites, is often unattainable.

When such is the case, it is best that, as has been suggested, it should be the reference reading room which is placed on the upper floor (Figs. 74, 75, and 76, Chelsea). Even if this room gains nothing in the way of light by such an arrangement, quiet is generally assured; and, provided that its existence is made sufficiently evident to the stranger by means of notices, it is a question whether the disadvantages really counterbalance the advantages. In fact, of recent years there has been a tendency, particularly in the case of large reference libraries, to place the main reading room at the top of the building. Indeed, if the library is on a sufficient scale to allow of an adequate lift service, the loss of accessibility is practically annulled, while, besides the advantages already mentioned, the greater facility for ventilation and the possibility of constructing the room without columns and such obstructions on the floor are considerations of no little weight.

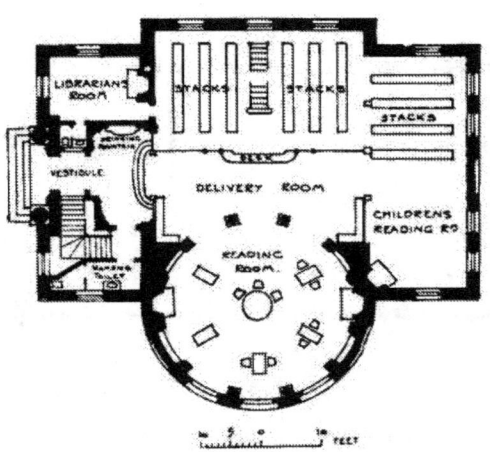

73. PUBLIC LIBRARY, WAYLAND, MASS.

Cabot, Everett, & Mead, Architects, Boston.

The whole question of the disposition of public rooms on different levels is one of great importance.

Generally speaking, the department which should be most accessible from the main entrance is the lending department.

There are usually, as has been said, certain hours of the day when borrowers come in great numbers, and at such hours, especially since they themselves are often pressed for time, it is most important that they should be got out of the building again as quickly as possible to make room for others.

For every reason it is important that the coming and going of the

PRINCIPLES OF PUBLIC LIBRARY DESIGN.

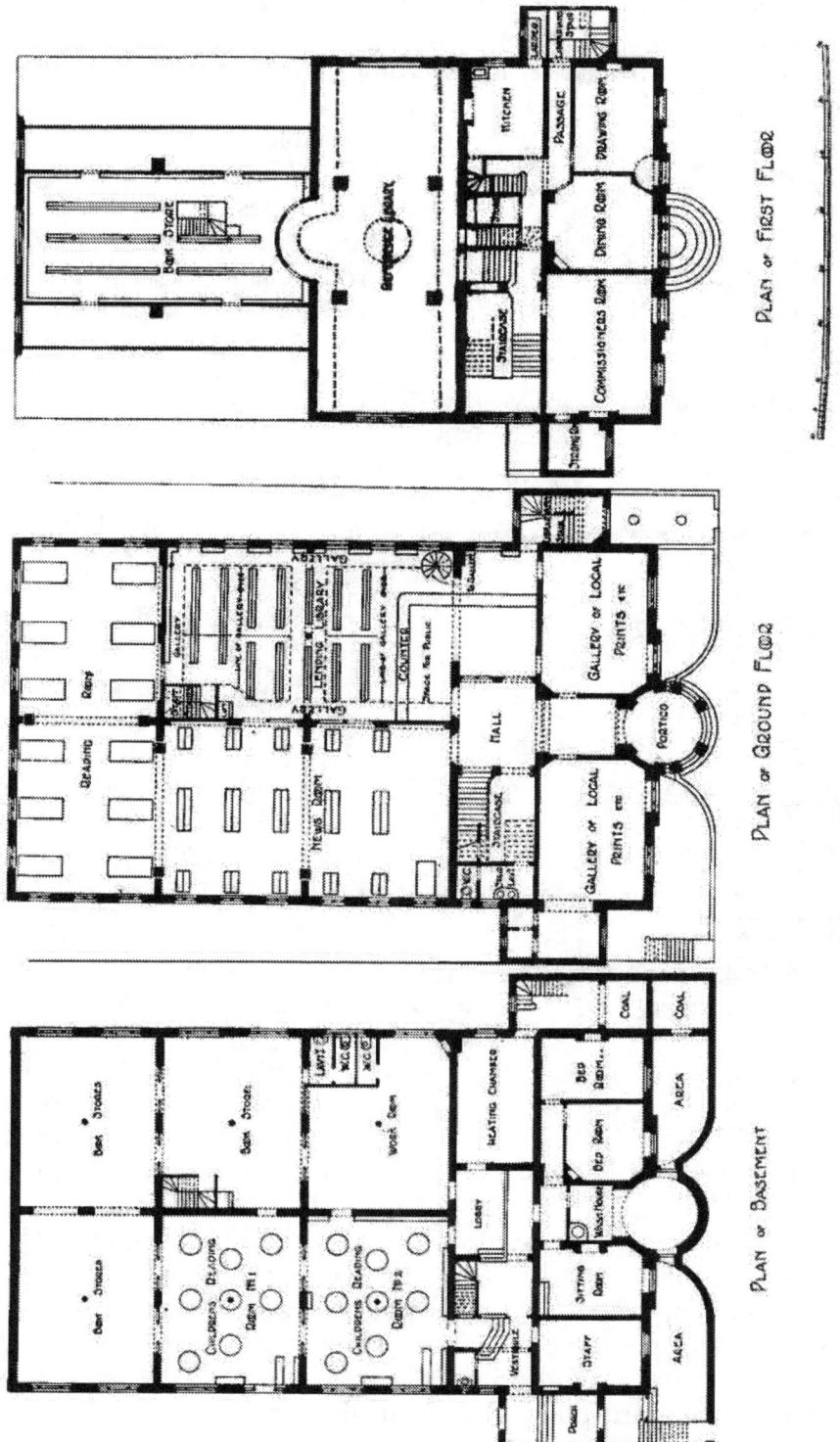

74, 75, AND 76. CHELSEA PUBLIC LIBRARY.

The late J. M. Brydon, F.R.I.B.A., Architect.

borrowers should occupy as little space and time as possible, and they should certainly not have to crowd up and down a staircase. There can, therefore, be no hesitation in asserting that, as a general rule, this department before all should be as near the entrance and exit as possible.

The next most important in respect of accessibility are the periodical reading rooms, and especially those devoted to newspapers.

The newspaper reader is not usually in such a hurry as the borrower: very often, as has been said, he is a professional loafer, and generally a flush time in a periodical room is an altogether more leisurely affair than in the lending department. At the same time, the coming and going to and from these rooms is more continuous and, therefore, a more fertile source of noise and confusion: so much so, indeed, that the accessibility of the news-room is sometimes considered of greater moment than that of the lending department (Figs. 77 and 78); while there may, of course, be other considerations in particular instances which favour the placing of such reading rooms, rather than the lending library, on the ground floor.

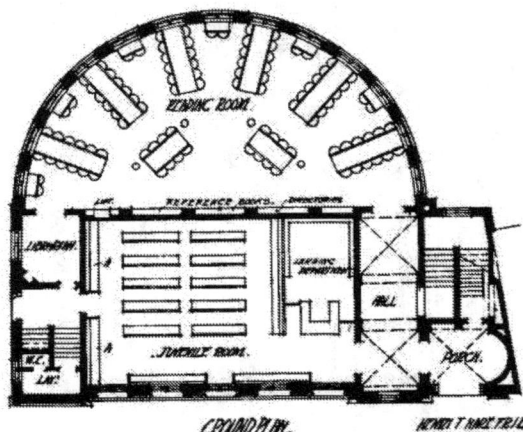

77 AND 78. ISLINGTON PUBLIC LIBRARY (NORTH BRANCH).

H. T. Hare, F.R.I.B.A., *Architect.*

Ladies' reading rooms, where these are adopted, are merely a further subdivision of the periodical room, and are subject to the same considerations in respect of location.

Juvenile rooms are often placed at the top of the building, as children do not mind having to climb stairs; but stairs to a juvenile department are undeniably a great disadvantage from the point of view of supervision, and, as has been already pointed out, a basement is for many reasons a better situation for this department than an upper floor. Lecture rooms may also, as has been said, under certain conditions be placed in a basement (see p. 101).

When lecture rooms are used for lectures or meetings during the hours when the library is open, they should be as far as possible from the reading rooms; and, even if they can be entered through the library entrance, there should always be a separate door for use when occasion requires.

The best position for such rooms as reference reading rooms, which require most of all quiet and light, and to which accessibility is of less importance than isolation, is, as has been indicated, the highest floor of the building, though generally this should not be higher than a first floor.

Where, therefore, the public accommodation of a library has to be divided between two floors, the ground floor should generally contain the lending department and newspaper room, the first floor the reference department and possibly a magazine room. A third story should always be avoided unless there is one below the entrance level. In this case, the lending department would, for preference, be on the entrance floor with the reference department above, and the periodical reading room or rooms below it.

Such, then, are the main general considerations affecting the disposition of the public rooms. There remain those relating to the accommodation of the staff and to the administration of the library.

It is, of course, as necessary as in the case of the readers that the conditions under which the staff have to work should be in general as favourable as possible; that they should, for instance, have the benefits of pure air, a good light and a healthy aspect, and other conditions which to a great extent depend upon the location of the rooms they occupy. With regard to the relative positions of those spaces reserved for the staff on the one hand, and those for the public and the books on the other, the chief consideration affecting the question is that of economy of time. In other words, the best disposition of the various departments from the administrative point of view, and that which makes possible the greatest efficiency, is that which enables the staff to perform their duties with the least possible waste of time, and, therefore, that which makes the distances the shortest, more especially in the case of those which have to be very frequently traversed—for example, the distance between a delivery counter and a book store; while where one attendant has to serve either of two departments, as may be required, or even the whole library, it is, of course, important that he should be able to do so without having far to go. In this way very often the disposition of the building may modify the number of attendants required to work the library, while the concentration of the working space for the staff often effects a very real economy and one which should always be an object in designing a library.

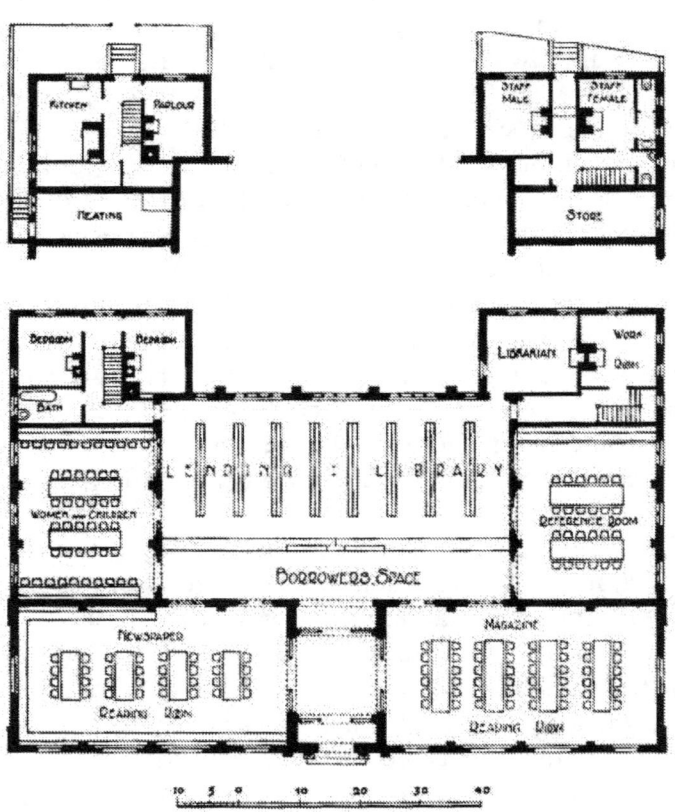

79. WAKEFIELD PUBLIC LIBRARY.
Alfred Cox, F.R.I.B.A., *Architect.*

The centre of the administrative activity of the library is usually the working space in the lending department, and except in large libraries, or where the public accommodation occupies more than one floor, this should, if possible, be a point more or less in touch with all departments (Fig. 79).

The position of delivery rooms, reference reading rooms, and special studies in relation to the book rooms, together with such collocations as that of the librarian's room with the working spaces on the one hand, and with the strong room and committee room on the other, have already been dealt with in the previous chapters.

There remains, however, one important consideration connected with the disposition of departments, namely, the need of what is generally known as supervision. There is, it may be thought, something rather aggressive in the term and its acceptance, and it is a pity that there is no more agreeable word. Though supervision is undoubtedly a safeguard against malefactors, and, as such, a benefit to the majority, the true spirit of it should be rather one of helpfulness, and the staff should be considered as allies to the readers, and not as spies.

Supposing that the staff is small and occupied exclusively in the working space of the lending department, it is important that this point should command at any rate the entrances and exits, the entrance hall and part at least of the reading rooms: certainly, as far as possible, ladies' and children's rooms. The value of such an arrangement lies at least as much in the fact that it gives opportunities for valuable assistance as in its power as a deterrent; and both of these results are just as much due to the fact that the attendants can be seen by the public, as to the fact that the public can be seen by the attendants; perhaps, indeed, more so, since library work seldom gives opportunities for looking about. Of course, in large libraries attendants have to be stationed in other parts of the building: in the reference library, for instance, or sometimes in the periodical room or juvenile rooms; while there is often a porter who can supervise the entrances from a box and visit the various departments from time to time in order to put up fresh papers and set straight misplaced magazines, to open and shut windows, turn up lights, and so on. The porter has, however, occasionally to leave his post in order to attend to the heating apparatus, or for some other purpose, and the attendants in various rooms have to get their meals. Consequently, it is important in any case—though, of course, where the public rooms occupy two or more floors it is impossible to obtain supervision of the whole from one point—that the working space in the lending library, where some one has always to be in charge, should occupy more or less a position of command.

It is, at the same time, only too common a thing to see library plans which illustrate an utterly ill-proportioned conception of the meaning and needs of supervision. Every convenience is sacrificed at the shrine of "supervision." Often the "librarian's office" is the centre of it, and lines are drawn on the plan from his desk to every corner of the building to show, apparently, that he can see all ways at once and has nothing better to do than to show off this unusual accomplishment.

The substitution of glazed screens for solid partition walls (Fig. 80) in library buildings is to a large extent due to the need, real or imaginary, of supervision. Since they are also incidentally an assistance to the lighting of the building, their use may be recommended within certain limitations. They should never, for instance, be used where a solid wall would ensure more quiet in a reference reading room, or students' room, or librarian's office. The occasion on which their use is to be most strongly advocated is in branch libraries where the whole attendance may devolve on one person, and here more especially when there is no considerable reference library. In such cases, indeed, even screens may be abolished, and the space divided by low barriers only (*cf.* Figs. 99 and 100). The amount of supervision required will depend largely on the locality, it being always remembered that the least conscientious class in a library are very often the idle women of the upper middle class.

The question of economy is a very important one and will be further discussed in the next chapter. As it affects the disposition of the rooms, it is very often a fact that the plan which is most economical in cost of building is also most economical in working. This must not, however, be taken as a recommendation to parsimoniousness, for that is the worst enemy of library work, and it must always be remembered that to save in cost of building at the expense of efficiency must be a very false economy. Rather that simplicity and straightforwardness of planning which is nearly always the surest road to a workable building,

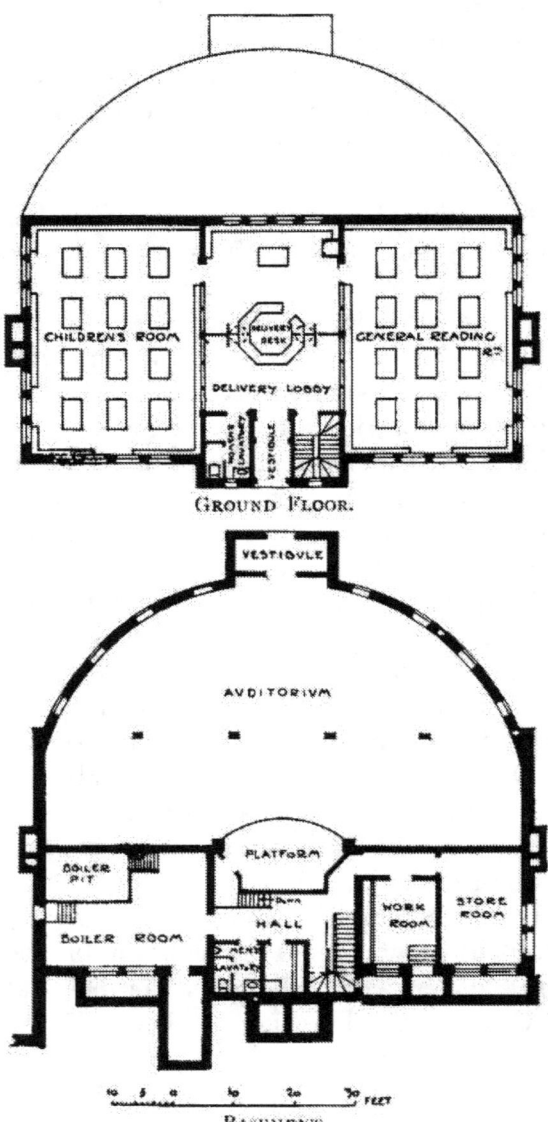

80 AND 81. CARNEGIE LIBRARY, HAZELWOOD BRANCH, PITTSBURG, PA.

Alden & Harlow, Architects.

82. CHELSEA PUBLIC LIBRARY.

The late John Brydon, F.R.I.B.A., Architect.

83. ISLINGTON CENTRAL LIBRARY.

H. T. Hare, F.R.I.B.A., Architect.

with a minimum of awkward angles, useless corners, meretricious eccentricities and wastefulness generally, should be the predominant characteristic of library design.

There remains to be considered the question of possible future extensions. This is a matter in regard to which it is almost impossible to particularise. Generally the nature of the extension (that is to say, whether the added accommodation will be for readers or books, or for other purposes) and its probable extent should be first ascertained, and when this has been done the complete scheme should be planned as a whole. If the part immediately required is first designed alone, the remainder has usually to be fitted on as best it may, and the result is seldom a workable whole.

As has been already shown, the extension of municipal public libraries is largely effected by the establishment of branches. It is, however, not infrequently necessary (especially in the case of the central, where this contains the reference stock for the whole system) to allow for some increase in storage capacity; while sometimes the addition in the future of a museum and art gallery, or a lecture hall, is contemplated. The arrangement of such heterogeneous accommodation is, as has already been pointed out, a matter in which none but general rules can be laid down. With regard to museums and art galleries it is generally advisable that these should be so placed that they may be readily accessible to the reference readers, more especially if the objects they contain are particularly associated with any special collections in that department. Their position should not, however, be such as to involve disturbance to readers from the coming and going of the curious.

Whether separate entrances should or should not be provided must depend entirely upon particular circumstances and the system in use. Generally one entrance to the whole building is preferable to two or a number, as it allows of more easy supervision; though if the museums or art galleries are open for lectures or meetings at times when the library proper is closed, a separate entrance must be provided. This can, of course, be closed when it is desired that the library entrance only shall be used.

When the library forms part of the municipal offices, it should, of course, be compact and complete in itself, with, for preference, a separate entrance from the outside.

Æsthetic Treatment.—The æsthetic treatment of public library buildings is a matter for which it is obviously impossible to lay down hard and fast rules. It must not therefore be supposed that under the present head any suggestion will be made as to the adoption of any particular style. Such a suggestion would be as useless as undesirable, and only a few general considerations affecting this question will be discussed.

While it is undeniable that the more directly utilitarian requirements should always take precedence, the æsthetic treatment of a public library building is no unimportant matter. The appearance of the fabric, within and without, should not be merely passively compatible with utility, but should actively assist it. This it may do in three ways. In the first place, a building which is a work of art is in itself a powerful educational factor; in the second, a dignified structure commands respect for the work with which it is associated; while, lastly, an attractive exterior and pleasing interior are great inducements towards the use of the building.

With regard to the educational value of a concrete example of good taste, that an acquaintance with what is good in art leads to a general recognition of the difference between the good and the bad will hardly be denied: indeed, this educational function would seem peculiarly appropriate in the case of a building devoted to an essentially educational purpose.

The second point, namely, the respect instilled by a dignified structure, is perhaps somewhat more tangible. There is no doubt that the public behaves itself better in an attractive and well-equipped building than in a barrack, and that it is more likely to educate itself in rooms which look as if they were intended for such a purpose than in those which rather resemble a third-class waiting-room at the railway station.

There is, however, considerably more in it than this. The library is for the public and belongs to the public, and if the fabric is such that the people can take a pride in their possession, the success of the institution is more than half ensured.

In this connection it may be noted that many library authorities seem to insist upon the term "Free Libraries." Such a title not only fails to indicate that proprietorship the recognition of which should considerably influence the attitude of the public towards these institutions, but it further conveys an unfortunate suggestion of soup-kitchens. The substitution of "Free" for "Public" seems altogether rather gratuitous. Municipal libraries are not constituted under "Free Libraries Acts," and the advertisement of the fact that no charge is made for admittance is quite superfluous. The inscription on the frieze of the public library, Boston, U.S.A. (Fig. 84), shows surely

84. BOSTON PUBLIC LIBRARY.

M'Kim, Meade, & White, Architects.

more of the right spirit towards an educational ideal than the laconic and somewhat condescending "Free Library" on so many English buildings.

American libraries seem to lapse less often into those utterly undignified suburban villa and public-house types which are only too common in this country. Possibly the very noticeable French feeling in American design is a little opposed to the characteristic restraint of what is best in English architecture, but there is no doubt that the public libraries in the United States are for the most part more dignified and more worthy of their purpose than those in this country.

To come to the final head, a striking and handsome exterior calls attention to the building and attracts visitors, while a comfortable and pleasing interior is an inducement to the use of the library. In this connection one important consideration must be noted, namely, that in the case of the interior decoration the treatment must be subordinated to the use of the building. Artistic effect must not be gained by means which cause inconvenience to the staff and distraction to the readers; nor, above all, should the decorations be such as to make the library a show-place for sightseers. At Boston, where crowds of visitors clatter continuously through halls paved with Istrian marble to gaze at decorations by Whistler, Sargent, Abbey, and others, reading is a matter of difficulty.

A reposeful dignity, a rather intangible but none the less real quality, should be the spirit of the internal treatment, and all display should be relegated to the exterior.

At the same time librarians usually accuse architects of spending too much of the money at their disposal on the exterior. In this they are no doubt very often right. It is, of course, true that the reader should have more consideration shown him than the passer by, potential reader though he may be. Many library buildings show little appreciation of this, having elaborately carved façades concealing bare and comfortless interiors. With many of them a limitation of the expenditure on the exterior would have rendered them less vulgar, though perhaps in these instances those within are to be congratulated on having less to suffer than those in the street.

Certainly the educational value, the dignity, and the attractiveness of many are as greatly impaired by vulgar extravagance as others by cheap ornamentation. With the rate limitation good proportion and restraint, which cost nothing, are the qualities which must be depended upon to give distinction to the exterior.

The reposeful dignity which should be aimed at in the design of the interior, though probably examples will occur to almost every one, is, as has been said, a somewhat intangible quality, and can only be negatively described, as being neither loud nor over-pretentious on the one hand, nor, on the other, mean and cheerless.

It has been said that no canon could or should be laid down as to what style or period is appropriate for a public library building, so long as it is not one which is uneconomical in cost or incompatible with the utility of the building, necessitating, for instance, on the one hand useless bay windows and turrets, on the other heavy mullions or narrow lights.

There are, however, so many famous library buildings of various dates in various parts of the world, that whatever style he adopts, the architect should not be at a loss to introduce, should he wish it, within or without, some happy reminiscence of a well-known example of library architecture.

85. REFERENCE READING ROOM, CHELSEA PUBLIC LIBRARY.
The late J. M. Brydon, Architect.

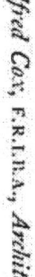

86. Kingston Public Library.

Alfred Cox, F.R.I.B.A., *Architect*.

87. BIBLIOTHÈQUE ST GENEVIÈVE, PARIS.
Henri Pierre François Labrouste, Architect.

Chapter XIV.

SINGLE LIBRARIES AND LIBRARY SYSTEMS.

HAVING considered the general principles which govern the planning of library buildings as such, it remains to point out how the application of these varies in particular instances according to the size of the library and the nature and extent of the accommodation it provides, whether these be conditioned by the income of the library, or, as is less often the case, by the extent of the population for whose use the library is intended.

For this purpose public libraries may be divided into two classes, those which are self-contained and complete in themselves, and those which form reciprocally complementary parts of a system of branch libraries, having, usually, a central library at their head.

Single Libraries.—When a new library is built in a given locality its size, and consequently its scope, is usually dependent upon the income from the library rate rather than, as should be the case, the number of persons likely to use it.

Occasionally, however, it is possible for the accommodation to be based on the population of the district. The following is a suggested calculation* for a town of 30,000 inhabitants, and is based on the best obtainable statistics relating to the use of British public libraries :—

Population		30,000
Borrowers, 6 per cent.		1,800
Reference readers, 4 per cent.	1,200	
Periodical readers, 10 per cent.	3,000	
Number of readers		4,200
Allow for one-half to use library daily		2,100
Library open twelve hours; 175 per hour for two departments.		

---

* I am indebted to Mr James Duff Brown for suggesting the accompanying table, and for the figures upon which it is based.

Accommodation to be provided*:—
- Periodical reading rooms, say - - - - - 120
- Reference reading rooms, say - - - - - 55
                                           ___
                                           175

An example of a library which bears such a relation to the population of the district in which it is situated is at Kettering, a town of about 28,500 inhabitants (Fig. 88).

Generally, however, the cost of the building is fixed and so dictates the extent of the accommodation. Attempts have been made to calculate the accommodation which can be provided by libraries with varying incomes,† and though such calculations are of necessity still more arbitrary than the figures on which they are based, they are a far better guide than if they attempted to establish relations on a basis of population in cases where this would be impracticable.

In such calculations the cost of building is an important factor.

---

* Borrowers do not stay in the library and only come as follows:—Fiction readers once in eight days, non-fiction readers once in twelve days: consequently they do not affect this calculation.

† Mr J. D. Brown's calculations are worth quoting as those of an experienced librarian, and as being the first real attempt hitherto at working out scientifically the capacity of a library building on the basis of its income.

Income.	Annual Repayment of Loan.	Building Loan.	Furniture Loan.	Cubic Feet in Building at 1s. per Foot.	Square Feet in Building.	Vols. Stored.	Readers Accommodated.
£	£	£	£				
1,000	250	3,600	400	72,000	4,412	34,000	200
2,000	500	7,200	800	144,000	8,824	68,000	400 (with branches).
3,000	750	10,800	1,200	216,000	13,236	102,000	600 (with branches).
4,000	1,000	14,400	1,600	288,000	19,200	136,000	800 (with branches).
5,000	1,250	18,000	2,000	360,000	24,000	170,000	1,000 (with branches).
10,000	2,500	36,000	4,000	720,000	48,000	340,000	2,000 (with branches).

The figures in the sixth column assume the building to be one story high, the height for purposes of the cube being taken as 15 feet, and the process by which the author arrives at the above figures are explained in the context (chapter vii.). These figures, he explains later (chapter viii., § 124), both as regards books and readers, can be con-

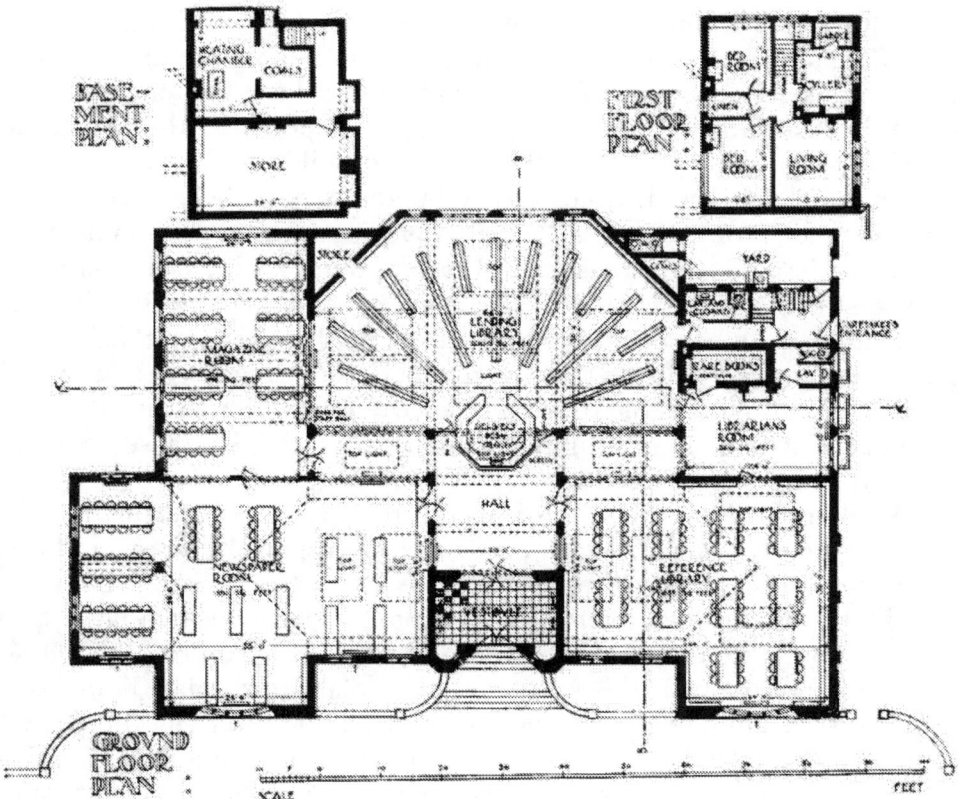

88. KETTERING PUBLIC LIBRARY.

Messrs Goddard & Sons, Architects.

As a general rule 1s. per cubic foot is probably about the right allowance in London considering that all possible fixtures are to be included; while 9d. or 10d., or less, is sometimes sufficient in the provinces. So siderably modified in actual fact, and gives the following suggestion as to the relations between income and stock.

Income.	Number of Vols. for which accommodation should be provided.
£500 to £1,000	20,000
1,000 ,, 2,000	40,000
2,000 ,, 3,000	60,000
3,000 ,, 4,000	100,000
4,000 ,, 5,000	130,000
5,000 ,, 6,000	160,000

Since the above appeared, the proportionate cost of buildings to income in the actual statistics has been reduced to 18 per cent. owing to the gifts of Mr Carnegie and others. Where, however, no donations affect the case, 25 per cent. may be considered a safe proportion.

great, however, is the variation in different instances, and according to the different circumstances, that it would seem impossible to attempt to draw any useful conclusion from a collation of selected examples.

Where a library cannot afford a sum of £4,000 or thereabout for building purposes, it is generally best not to build at all.

In many country districts library buildings have been erected at a cost of £2,000 or even less. Such libraries have to be administered by one underpaid and occasional librarian, often a girl, with assistance from a still more occasional charwoman or odd man, while the sum available for new books is infinitesimal. Usually about a third of the whole building is swallowed up by the periodical reading room, which in such circumstances is the only department which is in any way efficient; and the rather doubtful usefulness of this is not seldom considerably tempered by abuse.

With regard to the disposition of the various departments, this must depend, of course, in each particular case upon the shape and area of the site, and upon its surroundings.

There are, however, certain collocations of rooms which have been found not only economical but practically convenient, and on the bases of these one or two types of workable plans for small libraries of different sizes may be given, though it is obvious that in the case of libraries on more than one floor, or providing a large number of public rooms, the variety of the possible arrangements makes any classification impossible.

The simplest form of library which need be considered in this connection is a building containing two public departments. These would usually be a lending library and a reading room. In a small library of this type the whole building would be in charge of one person, who would be working mostly at the lending counter, and the arrangement illustrated (Fig. 89) places the whole library under his control.

In a library with three public rooms the same consideration applies; namely, the need of control by one person working at the lending library counter. In this case the extra room, which would probably be a small reference or magazine room, would be placed on the other side of the lending library, with the entrance in the centre of the whole building (Fig. 90). This type may again be still further expanded by the addition of one or two additional public rooms (Fig. 90, cf. Fig. 79).

Where the available income of a library is below £1,000, or the sum which can be procured for building less than, say, £3,600,

SINGLE LIBRARIES AND LIBRARY SYSTEMS.

exclusive of furnishing, it is better to rent premises which can be adapted more or less to the requirements of the library. These can often be obtained for a moderate rental which leaves a certain margin for the supply of literature, and thus enables the library to begin a useful if humble career, which is far preferable to pretentious futility.

As has been indicated above, the lending library, the reference department, and the periodical reading room are generally considered the essential elements of a public library. In library buildings costing from £4,000 to £6,000, these three departments,

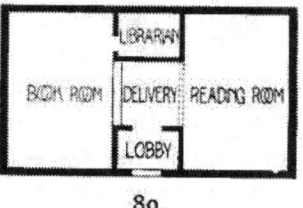

89.

together with a librarian's room and perhaps one staff room, will usually complete the scheme.

Beyond this, some such other departments as children's or women's rooms may be added, or the periodical room may be divided into two, one room for magazines, and one for newspapers (see Figs. 79 and 88), though the addition of a lecture room rather than any of these will probably recommend itself to modern ideas.

Not infrequently, too, the somewhat wasteful luxury of a librarian's residence is added to the initial cost. A caretaker's residence is to be preferred (see Fig. 79), while the remaining staff accommodation increases proportionately. Where there is more money still, the addition of exhibition galleries or lecture rooms is to be recommended, the former being often very useful in connection with a good reference library.

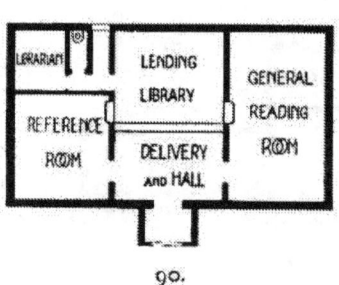

90.

In many cases, of course, even in libraries on one floor, the adoption of the types illustrated is impossible, and there are many other ingenious though straightforward collocations (see Fig. 72).

91.

One other type of library is so frequent and so often necessitated by extraneous conditions as to need special mention.

When the site is too narrow for the arrangement already described, a usual method is to place the lending library in the front of the building, and the periodical room and reference room at the back (Figs. 92 and 93). A short corridor, extending for the width of the lending library, gives access to the periodical room, which must, in this case, be used as a passage to the reference room.

There is, of course, some disadvantage in making one department a thoroughfare to another, but where a site is cramped, an ideal arrangement is often impossible. This plan, however, enables attendants working in the lending department to supervise and serve those in the other rooms, and it also gives fair control of the entrance corridor. The lending library, having good light from the front, can be built

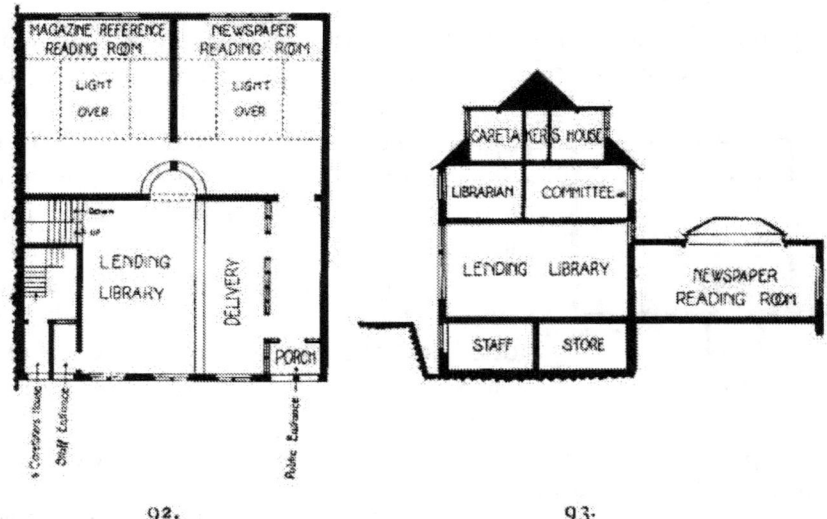

92.   93.

over, and often has a basement containing store-rooms and staff accommodation, while the back rooms can be top-lighted and are, more especially the reference room, exceedingly well placed from the point of view of quiet.

Here, too, there are, of course, many possible alternative schemes, but that described is generally, on the whole, the most satisfactory where the site is very cramped.

Library Systems.—When the library district covers a wide area, it is desirable to establish branches rather than to add to the central building.

The cost of the branches varies immensely in different districts

SINGLE LIBRARIES AND LIBRARY SYSTEMS.

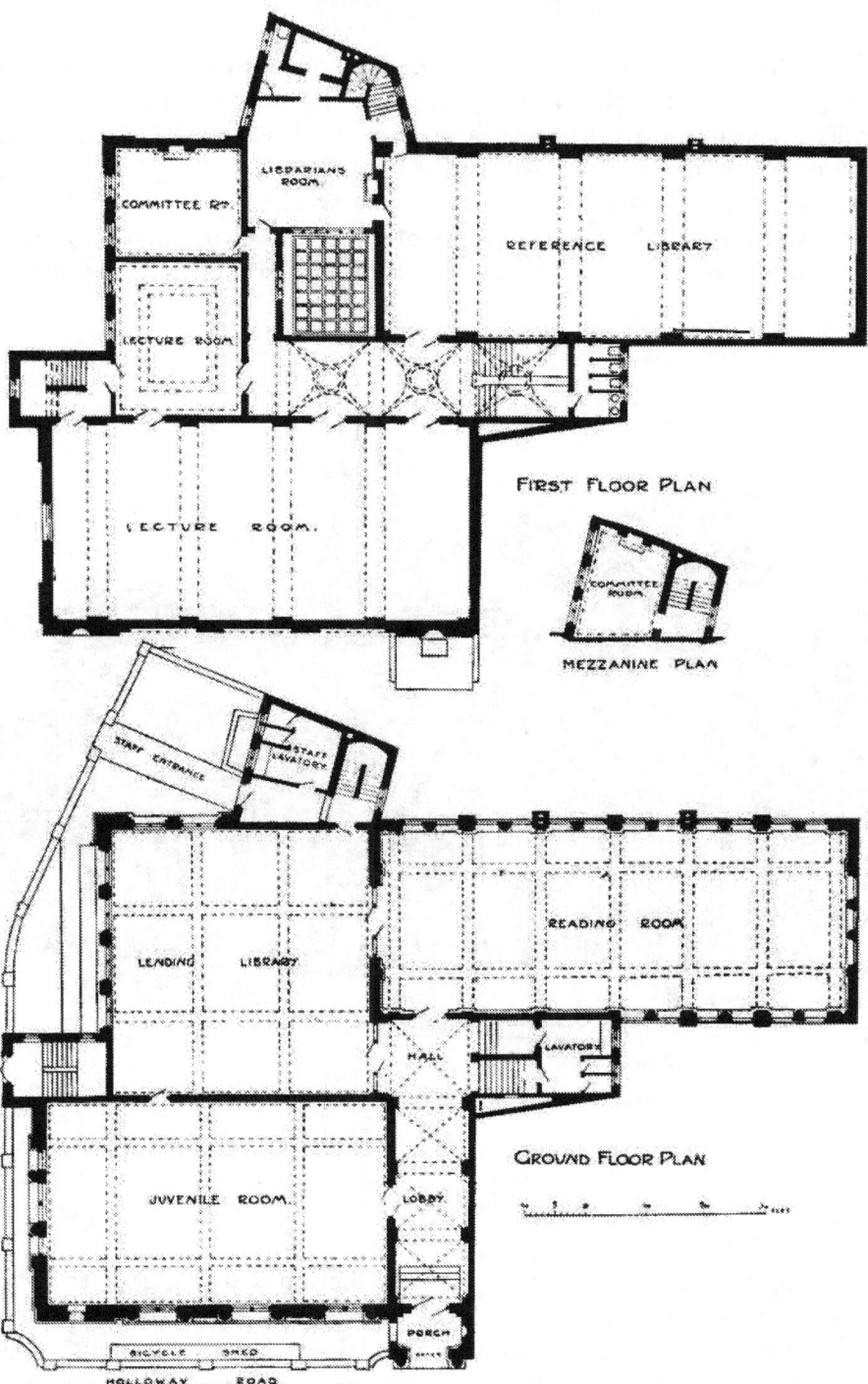

94 AND 95. ISLINGTON CENTRAL LIBRARY. (First Premiated Design.)
Henry T. Hare, F.R.I.B.A., *Architect.*

and in individual instances. There are, of course, means of distributing books through delivery stations in shops and so on, but generally speaking, no library with an income less than £1,500 should endeavour to build a branch library.*

Branch libraries are, of course, always worked in connection with the central, and usually an exchange of volumes is arranged between central and branches and between the different branches. It is at any

96. ISLINGTON CENTRAL LIBRARY.

H. T. Hare, F.R.I.B.A., *Architect*.

rate a great advantage for the catalogue of each library to include the stocks of all the others.

An important consideration in connection with the distribution of books is this, namely, that the value of a good reference stock is seriously diminished if it is scattered about in various buildings. Con-

---

* "Branch Libraries: their number and cost." By C. W. Sutton, M.A. (*Library Association Record*, vol. vi., No. 2.)

sequently, it is best that this should be kept complete at the central library, the branches being chiefly devoted to the delivery of lending books and the provision of periodicals. This arrangement is by no means invariable, but it is so obviously superior to others that under the subsequent heads of central and branch libraries only those which conform to this principle will be considered.

Central Libraries.—The central library is in the first place the home of the reference stock of the system, and the reference department is therefore the essential item of accommodation.

97. HACKNEY CENTRAL LIBRARY. (Second Premiated Design.)

Messrs Trimnell & Davison, Architects.

If it is on a large scale, it will usually consist of two main parts, a big reference reading room, often with supplementary rooms for special purposes, and a capacious book room. Generally, too, there will be periodical reading rooms, and often art galleries, lecture rooms, and so on (Figs. 94, 95, and 98).

In some cases there is no lending department attached to the central, this business being entirely relegated to the branches.

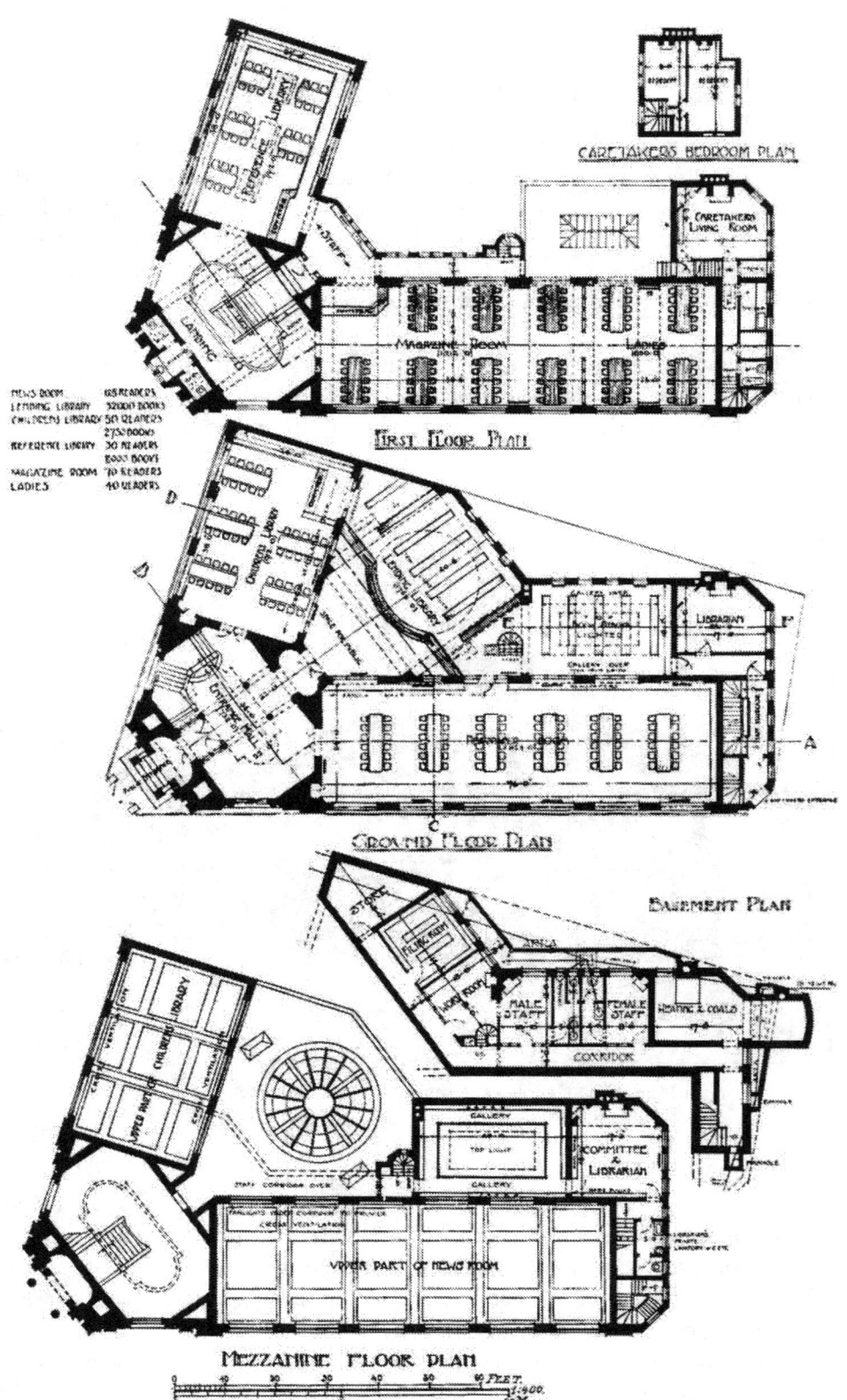

98. HACKNEY CENTRAL LIBRARY. (Second Premiated Design.)
Messrs Trimnell & Davison, Architects.

Generally, however, a central lending department is considered desirable.

Lastly, the central, as the administrative head-quarters of the system, must provide especially good accommodation for the librarian and staff, work-rooms, binderies, and so on, with sometimes separate offices for business connected with the administration of branches and the exchange service.

In small towns the central will not differ essentially from those libraries described under the last head, though it is important that

99. CARNEGIE LIBRARY, PITTSBURG, PA. (WEST END BRANCH).

space for the growth of the reference department and the business connected with the working of branches should be provided.

In large central libraries the accommodation of considerable stocks becomes an important matter. In America there are many libraries with very considerable stocks, and the stack system is usually adopted. The method of detaching the stacks from the main building has already been mentioned.* A more compact and less expensive arrangement is, however, generally to be preferred.

---

* Page 125.

PUBLIC LIBRARIES.

Branch Libraries.—As has been pointed out above, a reference department is not properly part of a branch library, though a few quick-reference books, such as directories and year-books, should, of course, be provided on shelves in the reading room. The lending library, though its stock should not generally exceed 15,000 volumes, is the most important department of a branch library, while usually one or two periodical rooms are provided; and a lecture room is nowadays beginning to be considered as an essential item of accommodation. The administrative accommodation required is generally small.

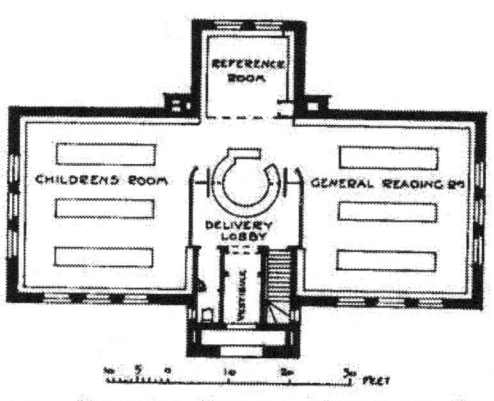

100. CARNEGIE LIBRARY, PITTSBURG, PA.
(WEST END BRANCH).

Alden & Harlow, Architects.

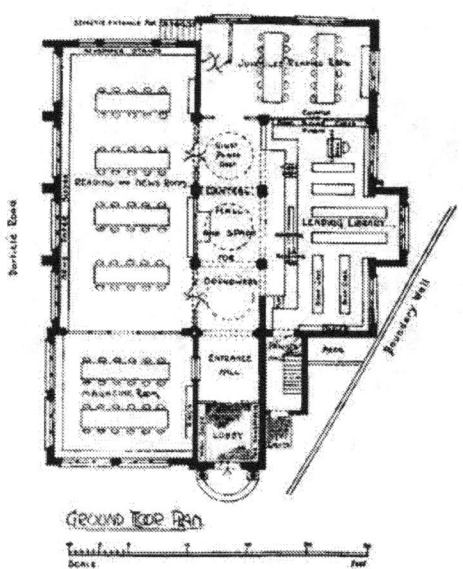

101. BROCKLEY BRANCH LIBRARY.

Albert L. Guy, F.R.I.B.A., Architect.

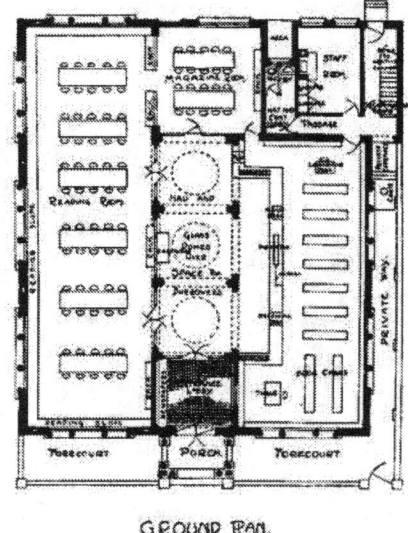

102. LOWER SYDENHAM BRANCH LIBRARY.

Albert L. Guy, F.R.I.B.A., Architect.

With regard to the best collocation of rooms in a branch library, this is a matter which, as has been said in connection with another class

SINGLE LIBRARIES AND LIBRARY SYSTEMS. 151

of building, is often of necessity modified by particular circumstances. Generally speaking, the types of small library given above (page 143) are applicable to branches. One or two examples showing useful arrangements and the accommodation of a typical branch library, have been illustrated (see Figs. 77, 78, 80, and 81).

Owing to the need of supervision, the abolition of solid internal walls, and even of glazed screens, in branch libraries is often necessary. Some American branches consist simply of one large room divided up by low barriers (Figs. 99 and 100).

Another requirement of branches in particular is simplicity of plan, and if possible a certain uniformity of arrangement throughout the system. Though absolute uniformity is generally impossible, owing to the exigencies of the site and for other reasons, yet a general similarity in the disposition of departments is very desirable (Figs. 101 and 102).

APPENDICES.

ACTS RELATING TO PUBLIC LIBRARIES.

APPENDIX A.

LIST OF ACTS OF PARLIAMENT RELATING TO PUBLIC LIBRARIES.

IRELAND.

1855. "18 & 19 Vict., c. 40. An Act for further promoting the establishment of Free Public Libraries and Museums in Ireland." (The principal Act.)

1877. "40 & 41 Vict., c. 15. An Act to amend the Public Libraries Act (Ireland), 1855."

1894. "57 & 58 Vict., c. 38. An Act to amend the Public Libraries (Ireland) Acts."

1902. "The Public Libraries (Ireland) Amendment Act."

Gives power to District Councils to adopt the Acts, and empowers County Councils to make grants in aid of libraries.

SCOTLAND.

1887. "50 & 51 Vict., c. 42. An Act to amend and consolidate the Public Libraries (Scotland) Acts." (The principal Act.)

1894. "57 & 58 Vict., c. 20. An Act to amend the Public Libraries Consolidation (Scotland) Act, 1887."

1899. "62 & 63 Vict., c. 5. An Act to amend the Public Libraries (Scotland) Acts."

ENGLAND AND WALES.

1892. "55 & 56 Vict., c. 53. An Act to consolidate and amend the law relating to Public Libraries." (The principal Act.)

1893. "56 Vict., c. 11. An Act to amend the Public Libraries Act, 1892."

1898. "61 & 62 Vict., c. 53. An Act to provide for the Punishment of Offences in Libraries."

1901. "1 Edw. 7. An Act to amend the Acts relating to Public Libraries, Museums and Gymnasiums, and to regulate the liability of managers of libraries to proceedings for libel."

[NOTE.—This Act does *not* deal with actions for libel. It was originally intended to do so, but the clauses were struck out of the bill, and the title escaped emendation.

SUMMARY OF PROVISIONS OF LIBRARIES ACT.

(*a*) ADOPTION OF ACTS IN TOWNS.—The Acts may be adopted in any city, county borough, burgh or urban district by a resolution passed by the council, at a special meeting of which a month's notice shall have been given, and the resolution must be advertised publicly in the usual way, and a copy sent to the Local Government Board, if the adoption is in England or Ireland; while a notice of the fact of adoption must also be sent.

(*b*) ADOPTION OF ACTS IN PARISHES.—In parishes in England and Scotland the Acts can only be adopted by a majority vote of the householders or voters.

(*c*) LIBRARY RATE.—A rate of one penny in the £ on the rateable value of an administrative area is the limit fixed by the Act, but power is given to parishes to fix a smaller sum by a popular vote, and to urban districts of all kinds to remove or fix any rate within the limit of one penny by resolution of the council.

(*d*) POWERS.—The Library Authority may provide public libraries, museums, schools for science, art galleries and schools for art, and for that purpose may purchase and hire land, and erect, take down, rebuild, alter, repair and extend buildings, and fit up, furnish and supply the same with all requisite furniture, fittings and conveniences. The Library Authority shall exercise the general management, regulation and control of every department established under the provisions of the Acts, and may provide books, newspapers, maps and specimens of art and science, and cause the same to be bound and repaired when necessary. Also appoint salaried officers and servants, and dismiss them, and make regulations for the safety and use of every library, museum, gallery and school under its control, and for the admission of the public thereto. Power is also given to make agreements with other library authorities for the joint use of library or other buildings; and to borrow money, with the sanction of the central authorities, for the purpose of buying sites, erecting buildings and furnishing them. The Irish Act of 1877 also gives power to establish schools of music as part of a library scheme.

APPENDIX B.

PUBLIC LIBRARIES ACT, 1892.
55 AND 56 VICT. CHAP. 54.

ARRANGEMENT OF SECTIONS.

ADOPTION OF ACT AND CONSTITUTION OF LIBRARY AUTHORITY.

SECTION
1. Extent and application of Act.
2. Limitations on expenditure for purposes of Act.
3. Proceedings for adoption of Act.
4. Act when adopted to be executed by library authority.
5. Constitution of commissioners for executing Act in parish.
6. Rotation of commissioners.
7. Meetings of commissioners.
8. Proceedings of commissioners to be recorded.
9. Power to vestries of neighbouring parishes to combine.
10. Power to annex parish to adjoining district.

EXECUTION OF ACT.

11. Provision of libraries, museums, and schools of science and art.
12. Provision as to acquisition and disposal of land.
13. Power to grant charity land for purposes of this Act.
14. Vesting of property in library authority.
15. Management of libraries, &c., by library authority or committee.
16. Power to library authorities to make agreements for use of library.
17. Power to library authority to accept parliamentary grant.

FINANCIAL PROVISIONS.

18. Expenses of library authority how defrayed.
19. Borrowing by library authority.
20. Accounts and audit.

PROVISIONS AFFECTING LONDON ONLY.

21. Application of Act to City of London.
22. Power for district in London to adopt Act.
23. Power to vestry or district board in London to appropriate land for library, &c.

SUPPLEMENTAL PROVISIONS.

24. Adjustment of interests on termination of agreement.
25. Saving for Oxford.
26. Constitution and proceedings of vestry for purposes of Act.
27. Definitions.
28. Repeal.
29. Saving as to local Acts.
30. Commencement.
31. Short title.
   SCHEDULES.

APPENDIX B.

An Act to Consolidate and Amend the Law relating to Public Libraries [27th June 1892].

Be it enacted by the Queen's most Excellent Majesty, by and with the advice and consent of the Lords Spiritual and Temporal, and Commons, in this present Parliament assembled, and by the authority of the same, as follows:—

Adoption of Act and Constitution of Library Authority.

<small>Extent and application of Act.</small>

1.—(1.) This Act shall extend to every library district for which it is adopted.

(2.) For the purposes of this Act, and subject to the provisions thereof, every urban district and every parish in England and Wales which is not within an urban district, shall be a library district.

(3.) This Act shall have effect as regards any parish which is partly within and partly without an urban district, as if the part which is without the district were a separate parish, and the overseers for the parish shall be deemed for the purposes of this Act to be the overseers for that part.

<small>Limitations on expenditure for purposes of Act.</small>

2.—(1.) A rate or addition to a rate shall not be levied for the purposes of this Act for any one financial year in any library district to an amount exceeding one penny in the pound.

(2.) This Act may be adopted for any library district, subject to a condition that the maximum rate, or addition to a rate, to be levied for the purposes of this Act in the district, or in any defined portion of the district, in any one financial year, shall not exceed one halfpenny or shall not exceed three farthings in the pound, but such limitation if fixed at one halfpenny may be subsequently raised to three farthings or altogether removed, or where it is for the time being fixed at three farthings may be removed.

3. With respect to—
   - (*a*) the adoption of this Act for any library district; and
   - (*b*) the fixing, raising, and removing of any limitation on the maximum rate to be levied for the purposes of this Act; and
   - (*c*) the ascertaining of the opinion of the voters with respect to any matter for which their consent is required under this Act;

the following provisions shall have effect; that is to say,

   (1.) Any ten or more voters in the library district may address a requisition in writing to the authority hereafter in this section mentioned requiring that authority to ascertain the opinion of the voters in the district with respect to the question or questions stated in the requisition: Provided that where the library district is a municipal borough the requisition may be made by the council of the borough:

(2.) On receipt of the requisition the said authority shall proceed to ascertain by means of voting papers the opinion of the voters with respect to the said question or questions; but the said authority shall not ascertain the opinion of the voters on any question with respect to the limitation of the rate unless required to do so by the requisition, or with respect to any limitation of the rate other than the limitations specified in this Act:

(3.) The procedure for ascertaining the opinion of the voters shall be in accordance with the regulations contained in the First Schedule to this Act; and those regulations shall have effect as if they were enacted in the body of this Act:

(4.) Every question so submitted to the voters shall be decided by the majority of answers to that question recorded on the valid voting papers, and where the majority of those answers are in favour of the adoption of this Act, the same shall forthwith, on the result of the poll being made public, be deemed to be adopted:

(5.) Where the opinion of the voters in any library district is ascertained upon the question as to the adoption of this Act, or upon a question as to the limitation of the rate, no further proceeding shall be taken for ascertaining the opinion of the voters until the expiration of one year at least from the day when the opinion of the voters was last ascertained, that is to say, the day on which the voting papers were collected:

(6.) The authority to ascertain the opinion of the voters for the purposes of this section shall be in a municipal borough the mayor, and in any other urban district the chairman of the urban authority, and in a parish the overseers.

4. This Act when adopted for any library district shall be carried into execution, if the library district is an urban district by the urban authority, and, if it is a parish, by the commissioners appointed under this Act; and any such authority or commissioners executing this Act are hereinafter referred to as a "library authority." *Act when adopted to be executed by library authority.*

5.—(1.) Where this Act is adopted for any parish the vestry shall forthwith appoint not less than three or more than nine voters in the parish to be commissioners for carrying this Act into execution. *Constitution of commissioners for executing Act in parish.*

(2.) The commissioners shall be a body corporate by the name of "The Commissioners for Public Libraries and Museums for the parish of   , in the county of   ," and shall have perpetual succession and a common seal, with power to acquire and hold lands for the purposes of this Act, without any licence in mortmain.

Rotation of commissioners.

6.—(1.) The commissioners shall, as soon as conveniently may be after their appointment, divide themselves by agreement, or in default of agreement by ballot, into three classes, one third, or as nearly as may be one third of them, being in each class.

(2.) The offices of the first class shall be vacated at the expiration of one year, the offices of the second class at the expiration of two years, and the offices of the third class at the expiration of three years from the time of their appointment.

(3.) The offices of vacating commissioners shall be filled by an equal number of new commissioners to be appointed by the vestry from among the voters in the parish; and every newly elected commissioner shall hold his office for the term of three years from the date when the office became vacant, and no longer, unless re-elected; but a person, on ceasing to be a commissioner, shall, unless disqualified, be re-eligible.

(4.) Any casual vacancy among the commissioners, whether arising by death, resignation, incapacity, or otherwise, shall as soon as may be after the occurrence thereof be filled up by the vestry; but the term of office of a commissioner appointed to fill up a casual vacancy shall expire at the date at which the term of office of the commissioner in whose place he is appointed would have expired.

Meetings of commissioners.

7. The Commissioners shall meet at least once in every month, and at such other times as they think fit, at some convenient place; and any one commissioner may summon a special meeting by giving three clear days' notice in writing to each commissioner, specifying therein the purpose for which the meeting is called. Business shall not be transacted at any meeting of the commissioners unless at least two of them are present.

Proceedings of commissioners to be recorded.

8. All orders and proceedings of the commissioners shall be entered in books to be kept for that purpose, and shall be signed by the commissioners or any two of them; and all such orders and proceedings so entered, and purporting to be so signed, shall be deemed to be original orders and proceedings, and such books may be produced and read as evidence of all such orders and proceedings upon any judicial proceeding.

Power to vestries of neighbouring parishes to combine.

9.—(1.) Where this Act is adopted for any two or more neighbouring parishes, the vestries of those parishes may by agreement combine for any period in carrying this Act into execution, and the expenses of carrying this Act into execution shall be defrayed by the parishes in such proportions as may be agreed on by the vestries.

(2.) The vestry of each of the said parishes shall appoint not more than six commissioners in accordance with the provisions of this Act, and the commissioners so appointed for the several parishes shall form one body of commissioners and shall act accordingly in the execution of this Act.

10. Where the voters in a parish adjoining or near any library district for which either this Act has been adopted, or the adoption thereof is contemplated, consent to such parish being annexed to the said district, such parish, subject to the consent of the library authority of the said district being also given, shall be annexed to and form part of that district for the purposes of this Act; the vestry of such parish shall appoint not more than six commissioners in accordance with the provisions of this Act, and the commissioners so from time to time appointed shall during their respective terms of office be deemed for all the purposes of this Act to be members of the library authority of the said district. *Power to annex parish to adjoining district.*

Execution of Act.

11.—(1.) The library authority of any library district for which this Act has been adopted may, subject to the provisions of this Act, provide all or any of the following institutions, namely, public libraries, public museums, schools for science, art galleries, and schools for art, and for that purpose may purchase and hire land, and erect, take down, rebuild, alter, repair, and extend buildings, and fit up, furnish, and supply the same with all requisite furniture, fittings, and conveniences. *Provision of libraries, museums, and schools of science and art.*

(2.) Where any of the institutions mentioned in this section has been established either before or after the passing of this Act by any library authority under this Act or the Acts hereby repealed, that authority may establish in connection therewith any other of the said institutions without further proceedings being taken with respect to the adoption of this Act.

(3.) No charge shall be made for admission to a library or museum provided under this Act for any library district, or, in the case of a lending library, for the use thereof by the inhabitants of the district; but the library authority, if they think fit, may grant the use of a lending library to persons not being inhabitants of the district, either gratuitously or for payment.

12.—(1.) For the purpose of the purchase of land under this Act by a library authority the Lands Clauses Acts, with the exception of the provisions relating to the purchase of land otherwise than by agreement, shall be incorporated with this Act. *Provision as to acquisition and disposal of land.*

(2.) The library authority of any library district which is an urban district, may with the sanction of the Local Government

Board appropriate for the purposes of this Act any land which is vested in that authority.

(3.) A library authority may with the sanction of the Local Government Board sell any land vested in them for the purposes of this Act, or exchange any such land for other land better adapted for those purposes, and the money arising from the sale or received by way of equality of exchange, shall be applied in or towards the purchase of other land better adapted for the said purposes, or may be applied for any purpose for which capital money may be applied, and which is approved by the Local Government Board.

(4.) A library authority may let a house or building, or any part thereof, or any land vested in them for the purposes of the Act, which is not at the time of such letting required for those purposes, and shall apply the rents and profits thereof for the purposes of this Act.

Power to grant charity land for purposes of this Act.

13.—(1.) Any person holding land for ecclesiastical, parochial, or charitable purposes may, subject as hereinafter provided, grant or convey, by way of gift, sale, or exchange, for any of the purposes of this Act any quantity of such land, not exceeding in any one case one acre, in any manner vested in such person.

(2.) Provided that—
- (*a*) ecclesiastical property shall not be granted or conveyed for those purposes without the consent of the Ecclesiastical Commissioners; and
- (*b*) parochial property shall not be so granted or conveyed save by the board of guardians of the poor law union comprising the parish to which the property belongs, or without the consent of the Local Government Board; and
- (*c*) other charitable property shall not be so granted or conveyed without the consent of the Charity Commissioners; and
- (*d*) the land taken in exchange or the money received for such sale shall be held on the same trusts as the land exchanged or sold; and
- (*e*) land situated in the administrative county of London, or in any urban district containing according to the last published census for the time being over twenty thousand inhabitants, which is held on trusts to be preserved as an open space, or on trusts which prohibit building thereon, shall not be granted or conveyed for the purposes of this Act.

(3.) Any land granted or conveyed to any library authority under this section may be held by that authority without any licence in mortmain.

14. All land appropriated, purchased, or rented, and all other real and personal property presented to or purchased or acquired for any library, museum, art gallery, or school under this Act shall be vested in the library authority. *Vesting of property in library authority.*

15.—(1.) The general management, regulation, and control of every library, museum, art gallery, and school provided under this Act shall be vested in and exercised by the library authority, and that authority may provide therein books, newspapers, maps, and specimens of art and science, and cause the same to be bound and repaired when necessary. *Management of libraries, &c., by library authority or committee.*

(2.) The library authority may also appoint salaried officers and servants, and dismiss them, and make regulations for the safety and use of every library, museum, gallery, and school under their control, and for the admission of the public thereto.

(3.) Provided that a library authority being an urban authority may if they think fit appoint a committee and delegate to it all or any of their powers and duties under this section, and the said committee shall to the extent of such delegation be deemed to be the library authority. Persons appointed to be members of the committee need not be members of the urban authority.

16.—(1.) The commissioners separately appointed for any two or more parishes for which this Act has been adopted may with the consent of the voters in each of those parishes agree to share in such proportions and for such period as may be determined by the agreement the cost of the purchase, erection, repair, and maintenance of any library building situate in one of those parishes, and also the cost of the purchase of books and newspapers for such library, and all other expenses connected with the same. *Power to library authorities to make agreements for use of library.*

(2.) The library authority of any library district may with the consent of the voters in the district and of the Charity Commissioners make the like agreement with the governing body of any library established or maintained out of funds subject to the jurisdiction of the Charity Commissioners, and situate in or near the library district, and, in case of inability, objection, or failure on the part of the governing body to enter into such agreement, the Charity Commissioners may, if they think fit, become party to the agreement on behalf of the governing body.

(3.) This section shall apply, with the necessary modifications, to a museum, school for science, art gallery, or school for art in like manner as to a library.

17. Where a library authority accepts a grant out of money provided by Parliament from the Department of Science and Art towards the purchase of the site, or the erection, enlargement, or repair, of any school for science and art, or school for science, or school for art, or of the residence of a teacher in any such school, or towards the furnishing of any such school, that authority may accept the grant *Power to library authority to accept parliamentary grant.*

upon the conditions prescribed by the Department of Science and Art, and may execute any instruments required by that Department for carrying into effect those conditions, and upon payment of the grant shall be bound by such conditions, and instruments, and have power and be bound to fulfil and observe the same.

Financial Provisions.

<small>Expenses of library authority, how defrayed.</small>

18.—(1.) The expenses incurred in a library district in and incidental to the execution of this Act, including all expenses in connection with ascertaining the opinion of the voters in the district, may be defrayed—

(*a*) where the library district is a municipal borough, out of the borough fund or borough rate, or a separate rate to be made, assessed, and levied in like manner as the borough rate; and

(*b*) where the library district is an urban district other than a borough, out of the rate applicable to the general expenses incurred in the execution of the Public Health Acts, or a separate rate to be made, assessed, and levied in like manner as the rate so applicable; and

(*c*) where the library district is a parish, out of the rate to be raised with and as part of the poor rate, subject, however, to this qualification, that every person assessed to the poor rate in the said parish in respect of lands used as arable, meadow, or pasture ground only, or as woodlands or market gardens, or nursery grounds, shall be entitled to an allowance of two-thirds of the sum assessed upon him in respect of those lands for the purposes of this Act.

(2.) Where the library district is a parish, and is not combined with any other parish for the execution of this Act, then—

(i.) such amount only shall be raised out of a rate for the purposes of this Act as is from time to time sanctioned by the vestry of the parish; and

(ii.) the vestry to be called for the purpose of sanctioning the amount shall be convened in the manner usual in the parish; and

(iii.) the amount for the time being proposed to be raised for the purposes of this Act shall be expressed in the notice convening the vestry, and (if sanctioned) shall be paid according to the order of the vestry to such person as may be appointed by the library authority to receive it; and

(iv.) in the notices requiring the payment of the rate there shall be stated the proportion which the amount to be thereby raised for the purposes of this Act bears to the total amount of the rate.

(3.) Where a parish or a part of a parish is annexed in pursuance of this Act to any library district, so much of the said expenses as is chargeable to such parish or part shall be defrayed in like manner as if such parish or part were a separate library district, but the sanction of the vestry shall not be required for raising the sums from time to time due from the parish for meeting those expenses.

19.—(1.) Every library authority, with the sanction of the Local Government Board, and in the case of a library authority being commissioners appointed for a parish, with the sanction also of the vestry of such parish, may borrow money for the purposes of this Act on the security of any fund or rate applicable for those purposes. Borrowing by library authority.

(2.) Sections two hundred and thirty-three, two hundred and thirty-four, and two hundred and thirty-six to two hundred and thirty-nine, both inclusive, of the Public Health Act, 1875, relating to borrowing by a local authority, shall apply, with the necessary modifications, to all money borrowed by any library authority for the purposes of this Act, as if the library authority were an urban authority, and as if references to this Act were substituted in those sections and in the forms therein mentioned for references to the Public Health Act, 1875. 38 & 39 Vict., c. 55.

(3.) The Public Works Loan Commissioners may in manner provided by the Public Works Loans Act, 1875, lend any money which may be borrowed by a library authority for the purposes of this Act.

20.—(1.) Separate accounts shall be kept of the receipts and expenditure under this Act of every library authority and their officers, and those accounts shall be audited in like manner and with the like incidents and consequences, in the case of a library authority being an urban authority, and of their officers, as the accounts of the receipts and expenditure of that authority and their officers under the Public Health Acts. Accounts audit.

(2.) The accounts of the receipts and expenditure of a library authority being commissioners appointed under this Act, and of their officers, shall be audited yearly by a district auditor in like manner and with the like incidents and consequences as in the case of an audit under the Acts relating to the relief of the poor, and those commissioners shall be a local authority within the meaning of the District Auditors Act, 1879. 42 & 43 Vict., c. 6.

(3.) The accounts of the receipts and expenditure under this Act of any library authority other than the council of a municipal borough shall be open at all reasonable times to the inspection, free of charge, of any ratepayer in the library district, and any such ratepayer may without charge make copies of and extracts from those accounts; and if any library authority or any person being a member thereof or employed by them and having the custody of the accounts fails to allow the accounts to be inspected, or copies or extracts to be made, as required by this section, such authority or person shall for each offence be liable on summary conviction in manner provided by the Summary Jurisdiction Acts to a fine not exceeding five pounds.

Provisions affecting London only.

Application of Act to city of London.

21.—(1.) The city of London shall be a library district, and on this Act being adopted for the city, the common council shall be the library authority.

(2.) The opinion of the voters in the city of London with respect to any question under this Act shall be ascertained by the mayor on the requisition of the common council.

(3.) The expenses incurred in the city of London in and incidental to the execution of this Act, including all expenses in connection with ascertaining the opinion of the voters, shall be defrayed out of the consolidated rate levied by the commissioners of sewers, or a separate rate to be made, assessed, and levied by those commissioners in like manner as the consolidated rate.

(4.) So much of this Act as limits the rate or addition to a rate to be levied in any library district for any one financial year to one penny in the pound shall not extend to the city of London.

Power for district in London to adopt Act. 18 & 19 Vict., c. 120.

22. Every district mentioned in Schedule B. to the Metropolis Management Act, 1855, as amended by any subsequent Acts, shall be a library district, and the provisions of this Act shall apply accordingly with the following modifications :—

(1.) The opinion of the voters in any such district with respect to any question under this Act shall be ascertained by the district board on the requisition in writing of any ten or more of such voters :

(2.) The library authority for such district shall be commissioners appointed by the district board, and the provisions of this Act relating to commissioners appointed for a parish shall apply with the substitution of "district" for "parish" and of "district board" for "vestry" :

(3.) The expenses incurred in any such district in and incidental to the execution of this Act, including all expenses in connection with ascertaining the opinion of the voters, shall to such amount as is sanctioned by the district board be defrayed by that board in like manner as if they had been incurred for the general purposes of the Metropolis Management Act, 1855, and the sums from time to time required for defraying those expenses, to the extent so sanctioned, shall be paid by the district board to any person appointed by the commissioners to receive the same ; but nothing in this enactment shall enable a district board to levy for the purposes of this Act any greater sum in any financial year than the amount produced by a rate of one penny in the pound, or any less rate specially fixed for the purpose of this Act in the district:

(4.) The enactments authorising two or more neighbouring parishes to combine in carrying this Act into execution shall have effect as if any such district were included in the term "parish" and the district board of such district in the term "vestry":

(5.) Where a parish in any such district has adopted the Acts hereby repealed or any of them, or hereafter adopts this Act, it shall be treated in all respects for the purposes of this Act as if it were outside the district, and, in particular,—

   (a) a person shall not, by reason of being a voter in the parish, be accounted for the purposes of this section as a voter in the district; and

   (b) a representative of the parish on the district board shall not take part in any proceeding of the board under this section; and

   (c) the parish shall not be called on to contribute to the payment of any expenses incurred in pursuance of this section; and

   (d) any question of accounts arising between the parish and the other parishes in the district, or between the parish and the district, in consequence of this section, shall be decided finally by the Local Government Board:

(6.) After the adoption of this Act for any such district, proceedings shall not, except with the sanction of the Local Government Board, be taken for the separate adoption thereof for any parish in the district.

23. The vestry or district board constituted under the Metropolis Management Act, 1855, for any parish mentioned in Schedule A. or district mentioned in Schedule B. to that Act, as amended by any subsequent Acts, may, if this Act is in force in such parish or district, appropriate with the sanction of the Local Government Board for the purposes of this Act any land which is vested in such vestry or board. *Power to vestry or district board in London to approximate land for library, &c.*

Supplemental Provisions.

24. Any agreement under this Act between two or more vestries or library authorities, or between a library authority and any other body, may provide that on the termination of the agreement an adjustment shall be made of the interests of the several parties thereto in any property to the provision of which they have contributed, and as to the mode in which the adjustment shall be arrived at, and in the event of any dispute the adjustment shall on the application of any *Adjustment of interests on termination of agreement.*

of the parties be made by an arbitrator appointed by the Local Government Board.

Saving for Oxford.

25. Nothing in this Act shall interfere with the operation of the Act of the session of the twenty-eighth and twenty-ninth years of the reign of Her present Majesty, chapter one hundred and eight, so far as it relates to the collection of a rate for a public library in Oxford.

Constitution and proceedings of vestry for purposes of Act.

26. For the purposes of this Act the vestry of a parish shall be any body of persons acting by virtue of any Act of Parliament as or instead of a vestry, and, where there is no such body, shall be the inhabitants of the parish in vestry assembled, but in the latter case the persons registered as county electors in respect of the occupation of property situate in the parish, and no other persons, shall be members of the vestry.

Definitions.

27. In this Act, unless the context otherwise requires—

The expression "urban district" means a municipal borough, Improvement Act district, or local government district; and "urban authority" means, as regards each such district, the council, improvement commissioners, or local board:

The expression "financial year" means the period of twelve months for which the accounts of a library authority are made up:

The expression "voter" means a person who is registered as a county elector or enrolled as a burgess in respect of the occupation of property situate in the district or parish in connection with which the voter is mentioned:

The expression "overseers" includes any persons authorised and required to make and levy poor rates in a parish, and acting instead of overseers:

The expression "common council" means in relation to the city of London the mayor, commonalty, and citizens, acting by the mayor, aldermen and commons in common council assembled.

Repeal.

28.—(1.) The Acts mentioned in the Second Schedule to this Act shall be repealed as from the commencement of this Act, save so far as any of them extend beyond England and Wales; and where those Acts have been adopted for any library district, that adoption shall be deemed to have been an adoption of this Act, and this Act shall apply accordingly.

(2.) For the purpose of this section the said Acts shall be deemed to have been adopted for any district in which they were in force immediately before the commencement of this Act.

Saving as to local Acts.

29. Nothing in this Act shall be deemed to limit, or to reduce or alter the limit of any rate which any library authority is authorised to levy under or by virtue of any local Act.

Commencement.

30. This Act shall come into operation on the first day of October next after the passing thereof.

Short title.

31. This Act may be cited as the Public Libraries Act, 1892.

SCHEDULES.

Section 3

FIRST SCHEDULE.
REGULATIONS FOR ASCERTAINING THE OPINION OF THE VOTERS IN A LIBRARY DISTRICT.

IN these regulations the expression "presiding officer" means, in relation to any library district, the authority required under this Act to ascertain the opinion of the voters in that district on any question, or a person appointed by that authority, and that authority is referred to in these regulations as the "district authority."

PART I.
PROCEDURE BY VOTING PAPERS.

1. The district authority shall, before the day appointed for the issuing of the voting papers, provide the presiding officer with a copy of the burgess roll or county register, as the case may be, or of the part or parts thereof containing the names of all the voters in the library district.

2. On the day appointed for issuing the voting papers the presiding officer shall send by post or cause to be delivered to every voter at his address appearing in the roll or register a voting paper in the form contained in Part II. of this Schedule or to the like effect.

3. Every voting paper shall bear the number of the voter on the roll or register, as the case may be, and shall contain directions to the voter, in accordance with these regulations, as to the day on which and the hours within which the voting paper is to be collected or sent, and as to the place at which, if sent, it will be received.

4. The district authority shall, before the issue of the voting papers, appoint such a number of competent persons as may be necessary to collect and receive the voting papers and to assist in the scrutiny thereof on such terms and for such remuneration as may be reasonable, and shall also appoint a convenient place within the district at which the voting papers are to be received, but the district authority shall not be required to collect any voting papers which have been sent by them to addresses beyond the limits of the district.

5. Voting papers shall be collected between 8 A.M. and 8 P.M. of the third day after that on which they were issued. Such day is hereinafter in these regulations referred to as the polling day, and such last-mentioned hour is hereinafter referred to as the "conclusion of the poll."

APPENDIX B.

6. A voting paper shall not after collection be delivered up to any person except the presiding officer or a person appointed to receive voting papers.

7. The persons appointed to collect the voting papers shall, either before or as soon as may be after the conclusion of the poll, deliver the voting papers collected by them to the presiding officer or to a person appointed to receive the same.

8. A voting paper may be sent by prepaid post or by hand to the presiding officer at the place appointed by the district authority for the receipt thereof, so that it be received by the presiding officer at such appointed place before the conclusion of the poll. Voting papers, except those collected by persons appointed by the district authority, shall not be received at the appointed place after the conclusion of the poll.

9. Every person appointed to collect voting papers shall be appointed in writing by the district authority, and shall carry such writing with him while employed in the collection, and shall show it to any voter who may require him to do so. If any person so appointed fails to comply with this regulation, or if any unauthorised person fraudulently receives or induces any voter to part with a voting paper, such person shall be guilty of a misdemeanour, and liable, on conviction, to imprisonment for a term not exceeding six months, or to a fine not exceeding twenty pounds, or to both imprisonment and fine.

10. A voting paper which contains the answer "yes" or "no" to any question put to the voters and is duly signed shall be deemed to be a valid voting paper with respect to that question.

A voting paper shall be deemed to be duly signed if signed by the voter with his full name or ordinary signature.

11. Where any voter is unable to write he may cause his voting paper to be filled up by another person. In such case he shall attach his mark to the voting paper, and such mark shall be attested by such other person, who shall sign his name and append his address thereto. A voting paper to which such mark is attached, and which is duly attested, shall be deemed to be duly signed.

12. Any person fabricating a voting paper, or presenting or returning a fabricated voting paper, knowing that the same does not bear the true answer or signature of the voter to whom it was sent or intended to be sent, shall be guilty of personation, and liable to the penalties of that offence, as provided by the Ballot Act, 1872.

35 & 36 Vict., c. 33.

13. The presiding officer shall, as soon as may be after the conclusion of the poll, proceed to a scrutiny of the voting papers, and shall compare the same with his copy of the roll or register, and ascertain how far the voting papers have been duly signed by the voters.

14. A question put to the voters shall be deemed to be answered and determined in the affirmative or negative, according as the majority of valid voting papers returned contain the answer "yes" or "no" to that question.

15. Immediately on the conclusion of the scrutiny the presiding officer shall report to the district authority the number of voters who have voted "yes" and "no" respectively to each question put to them, and the number of voting papers which are invalid.

16. The presiding officer shall seal up in separate packets the valid and the invalid voting papers respectively, and shall transmit them, together with his report, to the district authority.

17. Upon receiving the report of the presiding officer the district authority shall cause the result of the poll to be made public in such manner as they think fit.

Part II.

Form of Voting Paper.

Public Libraries Act, 1892.

BOROUGH (Parish or other Library District) of

No.   (Here insert number of voter in burgess roll or county register, as the case may be.)

Question 1	Are you in favour of the adoption of the Public Libraries Act, 1892, for the borough (*or* parish, *&c.*) of ?	Answer 1. (*To be filled in* "Yes" *or* "No.")	[To be omitted if Libraries Act already adopted.]
Question 2	Are you in favour of the rate being limited to one halfpenny in the pound? (*Or* to three farthings, *or* of the existing limitation of the rate under the Public Libraries Act, 1892, being removed, *or* of the existing limitation to one halfpenny being raised to three farthings, *as the case may require.*)	Answer 2. (*To be filled in* "Yes" *or* "No.")	[To be omitted if no question stated in the requisition as to limitation of rate.]
Question 3	Are you in favour of an agreement being made with (*here designate the body or bodies, according to section ten or section sixteen of this Act*) for the purpose of (*briefly state objects of proposed agreement*)?	Answer 3. (*To be filled in* "Yes" *or* "No.")	[To be omitted if no such question raised.]

                                                         Signature of Voter.

Note.

1. This voting paper will be collected by an authorised collector between the hours of 8 A.M. and 8 P.M. on   day, the 18 (*insert polling day*), or may be sent by prepaid post or

APPENDIX B.

by hand, addressed to (*state name or designation of presiding officer, and place appointed by the district authority*). If it is sent it must be received at that address before 8 P.M. on the above-mentioned day.

2. You may require the collector to show his authority in writing. No authority is valid unless it is (signed by *A.B., or* sealed, or *as the district authority may direct*).

Section 28.

SECOND SCHEDULE.

Acts Repealed.

Session and Chapter.	Short Title.
18 & 19 Vict., c. 70.	The Public Libraries Act, 1855.
29 & 30 Vict., c. 114.	The Public Libraries Amendment Act (England and Scotland), 1866.
34 & 35 Vict., c. 71.	The Public Libraries Act, 1855, Amendment Act, 1871.
47 & 48 Vict., c. 37.	The Public Libraries Act, 1884.
50 & 51 Vict., c. 22.	The Public Libraries Acts Amendment Act, 1887.
52 & 53 Vict., c. 9.	The Public Libraries Acts Amendment Act, 1889.
53 & 54 Vict., c. 68.	The Public Libraries Acts Amendment Act, 1890.

PUBLIC LIBRARIES AMENDMENT ACT, 1893.

An Act to amend the Public Libraries Act, 1892
[9th June 1893].

Be it enacted by the Queen's most Excellent Majesty, by and with the advice and consent of the Lords Spiritual and Temporal, and Commons, in this present Parliament assembled, and by the authority of the same, as follows:—

1. This Act may be cited as the Public Libraries (Amendment) Act, 1893, and shall be construed as one with the Public Libraries Act, 1892 (in this Act referred to as the principal Act), and these two Acts may be together cited as the Public Libraries Acts, 1892 and 1893. *Short title. 55 & 56 Vict., c. 53.*

2.—(1.) Where a library district is an urban district— *Modification as to adoption, &c., in urban districts.*

    (i.) The principal Act may, subject to the conditions contained in the second section of that Act, be adopted, and the limitation of the maximum rate to be levied for the purposes of that Act may within the limits fixed by that Act be fixed, raised, or removed, by a resolution of the urban authority under this Act:

    (ii.) The consent of the urban authority given by a resolution of that authority under this Act shall be substituted in an urban district for the consent of the voters in any case when the consent of the voters is required under the principal Act.

(2.) Section three of the principal Act is hereby repealed, so far as it relates to an urban district.

3.—(1.) A resolution under this Act shall be passed at a meeting of the urban authority, and one month at least before the meeting special notice of the meeting and of the intention to propose the resolution shall be given to every member of the authority, and the notice shall be deemed to have been duly given to a member of it, if it is either— *Provision as to a resolution of an urban authority for the adoption, &c., of the principal Act.*

    (*a*) given in the mode in which notices to attend meetings of the authority are usually given; or

    (*b*) where there is no such mode, then signed by the clerk of the authority, and delivered to the member or left at his usual or last-known place of abode in England, or forwarded by post in a prepaid letter, addressed to the member at his usual or last-known place of abode in England.

(2.) The resolution shall be published by advertisement in some one or more newspapers circulating within the district of the authority, and by causing notice thereof to be affixed to the principal doors of every church and chapel in the place to which notices are usually fixed, and otherwise in such manner as the authority think sufficient for giving notice thereof to all persons interested, and shall come into operation at a time not less than one month after the first publication of the advertisement of the resolution as the authority may by the resolution fix.

(3.) A copy of the resolution shall be sent to the Local Government Board.

(4.) A copy of the advertisement shall be conclusive evidence of the resolution having been passed, unless the contrary be shown; and no objection to the effect of the resolution, on the ground that notice of the intention to propose the same was not duly given, or on the ground that the resolution was not sufficiently published, shall be made after three months from the date of the first advertisement.

Power to two or more library authorities to combine.

4.—(1.) Where the principal Act is adopted for two or more neighbouring urban districts, the library authorities of those districts may by agreement combine for any period for carrying the Act into execution; and the expenses of carrying the Act into execution shall be defrayed by such authorities in such proportions as may be agreed on by them.

(2.) For the purposes of the Act a joint committee may be formed, the members whereof shall be appointed by the several combining authorities in such proportions as may be agreed on, but need not be members of any of the combining authorities. Any such committee shall have such of the powers of a library authority under the principal Act, except the power of borrowing money, as the combining authorities may agree to confer upon them.

(3.) Where any of the combining authorities are improvement commissioners or a local board the provisions of the principal Act with respect to accounts and audit shall apply to such committee as if they were a local board who were a library authority under the Act.

INDEX.

A

ACCOMMODATION in public libraries, *see under* Buildings, Size of, &c., *and* Departments, &c.
    Borrowers, for ; Readers, for ; Staff, for ; &c., *see under* Lending Libraries, Reading Rooms, Reference Department, Staff, &c.
ACETYLENE GAS, 14
ACTS—
    London Building Act—
        Public libraries defined as public buildings by, 5
        Stairs and staircases as required by, 8, 9
    Public Libraries Acts, 1, 157
        List of, 155
        Summary of, 156
        Text of (1892 and 1893), 157, 173
ADVERTISEMENT READERS, accommodation of, 104
ALCOHOL LAMPS, 14
AMERICAN LIBRARIES—
    Barrier libraries—
        Reference department of, arrangement of, 93
    Branch libraries, 151
    Catalogues in, arrangement of, 99
    Children's rooms in, 90, 91
ARCHITECTS—
    Public library movement and, 1, 2
    Selection and employment of, 119-122
AREAS—
    Required for—
        Public rooms generally, 22, 81, 83 ; magazine rooms, 87 ; children's rooms, 89
ART GALLERIES, 101, 102
    Entrances for, 135
ASPECT of library rooms, 10, 11

B

BARRIER SYSTEM—
    Lending libraries, in, *see under* Lending Libraries
    Reference libraries, in, *see under* Reference Department
BARRIERS, 60
    Fixing of, 6, 60
    Reference libraries, in, disposition of, 92, 93
    Substitution of, for internal walls, *see under* Partitions, Substitution of, &c.
BASEMENT, 5, 6
    Lighting of, 16
BICYCLE SHEDS, 103
BINDERIES, 107
BLINDS, 11
BOILERS, 26
BOOKCASES, 30-40
    Children's rooms, for, 91
    Construction and form of, 31, 32, 33, 35
    Dimensions of, 33, 34, 35, 36
    Disposition of, 61-64, 79, 97
    Doors for, 38
    Double and single, 31
    Dwarf, 38
    Folios, for, 39, 40
    Lending libraries, in,—
        Barrier system, 73
        Open shelf system, 79
    Materials for, 30, 31
    Reference department, in, *see under* Reference Department, Open Shelf Reference Libraries
    Revolving, 39
    Rolling 38, 39 ; use of, in book stores, 68
    Shelves for, 32, 33 ; movable, 37, 38
    Show-cases, 39 ; lending libraries (open shelf), in, 79 ; *see also* Exhibition Cases

BOOKCASES (*continued*)—
  Steps for, 35, 40, 41, 95, 96
  Storage, 38, 39
  Wooden, treatment of, 30, 31
BOOK ROOMS, 61-64
  Bookcases in, disposition and spacing of, 61, 62, 63, 64
  Circular and semicircular, 64
  Position of, 124
  Special subjects and collections, for, 97, 98
  Tables in, for students, 97, 98
  Windows in, arrangement of, 62, 63
BOOK SHELVES, *see under* Bookcases
BOOK STACKS, 64-67
  Central libraries, in, 150
  Construction of, 65, 66
  Decks of—
    Construction of, 65, 66
    Materials for, 66
    Number and arrangement of, 64, 65
  Height of, 64, 65
  Lifts in, 29, 67
  Lighting (artificial) of, 20, 21
  Lighting (natural) of, 66, 67
  Lightning conductors in connection with, 27
  Reference libraries (barrier system), in connection with, 93
  Stairs in, 66, 67
BOOK STORES, 67-69
  Heating of, unnecessary, 69
  Lighting of, 68
  Rolling bookcases in, 68
  Ventilation of, 69
BOOKS, space occupied by, 36
BORROWERS—
  Space for, in lending libraries (barrier system), 70, 71, 75, 76; *see also* Delivery Room
BOYS, separate accommodation for, 89
BRANCH LIBRARIES, 119, 150, 151
  Glazed screens used in, 134
  Income necessary for establishment of, 146
  Internal walls omitted in, 134
  Planning of, 127, 128, 150, 151
  Staff of, 134
BUILDINGS—
  Cost of, *see* Cost &c.
  Donations for, 116
  Expenditure on, 115
  Extension of, *see* Extension
  Purchase of, 116 (*note*)
  Rented, 117; *see also* 115 (*table*)

BUILDINGS (*continued*)—
  Size of—
    Income in proportion to, 114, 115, 116, 140, 141 (*note*)
    Population in proportion to, 139, 140
BYE-LAWS AND REGULATIONS, BUILDING—
  Doors, as to, 9
  Public libraries defined as public buildings by, 5
  Stairs and passages, as to, 8, 9

C

CARD CATALOGUES, *see under* Catalogues
CARD-CHARGING APPLIANCES, *see under* Charging Appliances
CARDS—
  Book, 57
  Borrowers', 57
CARETAKER, residence for, *see under* Staff, Accommodation for
CATALOGUES—
  American libraries, in, 99
  Card-catalogues, fittings for, 52
    Requirements of, room for, 99
  Combined, for lending and reference departments, 99, 100
  Fittings for, 51-53
  Lending libraries, in,—
    Barrier system, 73, 76
    Open shelf system, 79
  Placard catalogues, fittings for, 53
  Reference libraries, in, *see under* Reference Department
  Rooms for, 99-101
  Sheaf catalogues, fittings for, 52, 53, 99
CATALOGUING ROOMS, 107
CEILING LIGHTS, 13
CEILINGS—
  Colour of, 13
  Flat, preferable, 8
  Height of, *see* Public Rooms, height of
  Treatment of, 7
CENTRAL LIBRARIES, 147-150
CHAIRS—
  Children's rooms, in, 90, 91
  Reading rooms, for, 50, 51, 90
CHARGING APPLIANCES, 53, 54
  Cards, 56, 57
    Lending libraries, in—
      Barrier system, 74
      Open shelf system, 78, 79

CHARGING APPLIANCES (*continued*)—
  Cards (*continued*)—
    Trays for, 57 ; Counters for accommodation of, 58
  Indicators, *see* Indicators
  Ledger charging, 53
CHILDREN—
  Bookcases for, height of, 91
  Reading rooms for, *see* Reading Rooms, Juvenile Reading Rooms
  Tables and chairs for, height of, 90, 91
CHIVERS INDICATOR, 55, 56
CLASSIFICATION, SHELF, lending libraries (open shelf system), in, 79, 80
CLEANERS, sinks and cupboards for, 112
CLOCKS, 60
CLOSETS—
  Librarian's, 109
  Public, 102, 103
  Staff, for, 112, 113
  Women, for, 88
COAL GAS, 14, 15
COAL STORE, 112
COLLECTIONS, rooms for, 97, 98
COLOUR—
  Ceilings, of, 13
  Dado, of, 13
  Walls, of, 13
COMMITTEE ROOMS, 109, 110
  Floors of, 6
  Spare rooms used as, 102
COMPETITIONS, architectural, for public library buildings, 120-122
CONCERTS, spare rooms for, 102
CONVERSATION ROOMS, 101, 102
CORNICES, 8
CORRIDORS, 104
  Floors of, 6
COST OF PUBLIC LIBRARY BUILDINGS, 140, 141, 142
  See also under Buildings, Size of, &c., *and* Departments, &c.
COTGREAVE INDICATOR, 54, 55, 56
COUNTERS, 57, 58
  Charging trays, to accommodate, 58
  Dimensions of, where indicators used, 56, 58
  Ledger charging, for, 53
  Lending libraries, in,—
    Barrier system, 71, 72
      Indicators, with, 72, 73
      Indicators, without, 74, 76
    Open shelf system, 78, 79
  Newspaper rooms, in, 87
  Reference libraries (barrier system), in, 93, 95
CUPBOARDS, cleaners', 112

D

DADO, *see under* Walls, Internal Treatment of
DAMP, Exclusion of, 5, 6, 8, 124
DECKS, book stacks, of, *see under* Book Stacks
DECORATION, public library buildings, of, 137
DELIVERY ROOM, entrance hall used as, 105, 124, 125
  See also Borrowers, Space for, in Lending Libraries
DELIVERY STATIONS, 119
DEPARTMENTS to be provided in public libraries, 123
  Branch libraries, in, 150
  Central libraries, in, 147, 149, 150
  Disposition of, 123-135, 142, 143, 144
DESIGN of public libraries, 123-151
  General principles of, 123-138
  Library systems, 144-151
    Branch libraries, 127, 128, 134, 150, 151
    Central libraries, 147-150
  Single libraries, 139-144
DESKS—
  Movable, for ledgers, 53
  Reading, *see* Tables, Reading
DIRECTORY STANDS, *see* Stands, Directory
DISTRIBUTION of libraries, 119
DOORS, 9, 10
  Fireproof, 125
  Public entrances, in, 103, 104
DUST, Exclusion of, 7, 10, 124, 125
DWARF BOOKCASES, 38

E

EASELS, READING, 48
EAVES, 8
ELECTRIC HEATING, *see under* Heating
ELECTRIC LIGHTING, *see under* Lighting, Artificial
ELLIOT INDICATOR, 55 (*note*)
ENTRANCE HALL, 104, 105
ENTRANCES, 103-105
  Advertisement lobbies in, 104
  Children's, 89
  Doors in, *see under* Doors
  Galleries and museums, to, 135
  Lecture rooms, to, 131
  Lending libraries, to, 77, 78, 79
  Staff, for, 112, 113

EXHIBITION CASES, 43
 See also Bookcases, Show-cases
EXHIBITIONS, spare rooms for, 102
EXITS from lending libraries, 77, 78, 79
EXPENDITURE, *see under* Finance
EXTENSION—
 Planning with a view to, 124, 135
 Space for, 117

F

FANLIGHTS, 13
FANS, VENTILATING, 24
FICTION, Works of, 34, 80
 Indicators for, 72
FILES—
 Periodical—
  Racks for, *see under* Racks
  Stands for, *see under* Stands
FINANCE, 114-117
 Expenditure, items of, 114, 115
 Income—
  Accommodation in relation to, *see under* Buildings, Size of, &c., Cost of Public Library Buildings, *and* Departments &c.
  Sources of, 114, 116, 156
FIRE PREVENTION, 26-28
 Appliances for, 27
 Disposition of building in relation to, 27, 125, 126
 Fireproof construction, 5, 26
  Doors and shutters, 125
  Floors, 5
  Roofs, 8
  Walls, 7
 Lightning conductors, 27
 Safety lamps, 28
 Situation of building in relation to, 26, 27
 Water supply for, 27, 28
FIXTURES, loans for, 116
FLOOR SPACE for readers, 22, 81
FLOORS—
 Coverings for, 7
 Materials and construction of, 5-7
 Waterproof, 28
FOLIO CASES, 39, 40
FUEL STORES, 112
FURNITURE—
 Binderies, for, 107
 Cataloguing rooms, for, 107
 Committee rooms, for, 110
 Cost of, in relation to income and cost of building, 116, 117

FURNITURE (*continued*)—
 Expenditure on, 115
 Librarian's room, for, 109
 Loans for, 116
 Materials for, 42
 Mess-rooms, for, 110
 Miscellaneous, 60
 Reading rooms, in, disposition of, 81-84
 Workrooms, for, 106

G

GALLERIES, 41, 95, 96
 Art, *see* Art Galleries
 Magic lanterns, for, in lecture rooms, 101
GANGWAYS—
 Bookcases, between, 79
 Furniture of reading rooms, between, 83, 84
GAS, *see under* Lighting, Artificial
GIRLS, separate accommodation for, 89
GLASS—
 Prismatic, 13, 118
 Windows, for, 12, 13
GLAZED SCREENS, *see under* Partitions
GRATES, open, 24, 25
GUTTERS—
 Condensation, 13
 Long, to be avoided, 8

H

HAND-RAILS for staircases to children's rooms, 89, 90
HAT RAILS for chairs, 51
HEATING—
 Boiler and accessories, 25
 Book stores, of, unnecessary, 69
 Electricity, by, 17, 25
 Expenditure on, 115
 Fuel store, 112
 Heating chamber, 111, 112, 126
 Pipes and radiators, arrangement of, 25
 Systems of, 24, 25
 Temperatures required, 24

I

INCANDESCENT GAS, *see under* Lighting, Artificial
INCOME, *see under* Finance

INDEX.

INDICATORS, 54-56
   Arrangement of, in lending libraries, 72, 73
   Chivers, 55, 56
   Cotgreave, 54, 55, 56
   Elliot, 55 (*note*)
   Fiction, for, 72
   Periodicals and magazines, for, 56
   Size of, in relation to number of volumes registered, 56
   Unnecessary with small issues, 74
INSCRIPTIONS on public library buildings, 136, 137

J

JUVENILE ACCOMMODATION, 89-91
   Furniture for rooms, height of, 90
   Lending libraries, 89
   Position of rooms, 130, 131
   Reading rooms, 89-91

L

LADDERS, 41, 95, 96
LADIES' READING ROOMS, 88, 113
LAMPS, electric, arrangement of, 17-20
LAND, gifts of, 116
LANTERN LIGHTS, *see* Roof Lights
LANTERNS, MAGIC, 101
LATCHES, TREADLE, wickets, for, 59
LAVATORIES—
   Librarian's, 109
   Public, 102, 103
   Staff, for, 112, 113
   Women, for, 88
LECTURE ROOMS—
   Entrance to, 131
   Position of, 131
   Requirements of, 101
LECTURES, spare rooms for, 102
LEDGER CHARGING, 53, 54
LENDING DEPARTMENT, 70-80
   Barrier system, 70-76, 80
     Borrowers' space, 70, 71
     Counters in, 71, 72
     Disposition of, 71
     Indicators, with, 72, 73
       Bookcases in, 73
       Catalogues in, 73
       Counters in, 72, 73
     Indicators, without, 74-76
       Counters in, 74, 76
       Disposition of, 75, 76
     Staff accommodation in, 71, 75
   Lighting of, 20

LENDING DEPARTMENT (*continued*)—
   Branch libraries, in, stock of, 150
   Combination of open shelf and barrier systems in, 80
   Juvenile, 89
   Open shelf system, 76-80
     Bookcases in, 79
     Borrowers in, division of, 78, 79
     Catalogues for, 79
     Charging system in, *see* Charging Appliances, Card, Lending Libraries (open shelf system), in
     Counters in, 78, 79
     Entrances to, *see under* Entrances
     Exits from, *see under* Exits
     Lighting of, 20, 21
     Show-cases in, 79
     Staff accommodation in, *see under* Staff, Accommodation for
     Wickets in, *see under* Wickets
   Position of, 128, 130, 131
   Screens and partitions for, 126
   Working space for staff in, position of, 132, 135
LIBRARIAN—
   Residence for, *see under* Staff, Accommodation for
   Room for, *see under* Staff, Accommodation for
LIBRARY RATE, 114
LIFTS—
   Book, 28, 29, 67, 108
   Passenger, 29, 67
LIGHTING—
   Artificial, 14-21
     Acetylene gas, 14
     Alcohol lamps, 14
     Book stores, of, 68
     Coal gas—
       Direct use of, 14
       Incandescent, 14, 15
     Electricity, by, 15-21
       Advantages of, 17
       Basement light, 16
       Cost of, 15, 16
       Generation of, 15
       Lamps, arrangement of, 17-20
       Strong-rooms, of, 110
       Switches, disposition of, 20, 21
     Expenditure on, 115
     Petroleum lamps, 14
     Store-rooms, of, 69
   Natural—
     Binderies, of, 107
     Confined sites, on, 118
     See also Windows

LIGHTNING CONDUCTORS, 27
LOANS—
   Building, 114-117, 156
   Fixtures, for, 116
   Purchase of buildings, for, 116 (*note*)
   Sites, for, 115, 116, 156
LOBBY for advertisement sheets, 104
LOCAL GOVERNMENT BOARD, 116, 156
LONDON BUILDING ACTS, *see under* Acts

M

MAGAZINE READING TABLES, *see under* Tables, Reading
MAGAZINES—
   Indicators for, 56
   Racks for, *see* Racks, Current Magazines and Periodicals, for
   Reading rooms for, *see under* Reading Rooms, Periodicals, for
MAGIC LANTERN, provision for, in lecture rooms, 101
MAPS—
   Accommodation for, 42, 43
   Reference libraries, in, 93
MESS-ROOMS, 110
MUSEUMS, 101, 102
   Entrances for, 135

N

NEWSPAPER READING ROOMS, *see under* Reading Rooms, Periodicals, for
NEWSPAPER READING SLOPES, 48-50
   Advertisements, for, 104
   Window sills in relation to, height of, 12

O

OPEN SHELF SYSTEM—
   Lending libraries, in, *see under* Lending Department
   Reference libraries, in, *see under* Reference Department
OPEN SHELVES in children's rooms, height of, 91

P

PACKING ROOMS, 107, 108
PAINT—
   Ceilings, on, 7
   External woodwork, on, 8
   Washable, on walls, 8

PARTITIONS, 59, 60
   Glazed—
      Construction of, 59, 60
      Diffusion of light assisted by, 13, 59
      Height of, 59
      Substitution of, for solid partitions, 126, 133, 134, 151
      Supervision assisted by, 59, 133, 151
   Omission of, 126
PASSAGE ROOMS, 126, 127
PERIODICALS—
   Accommodation of, in reading rooms, 86, 87
   Indicators for issue of, 56
   Placard catalogues for, 53
   Racks for, *see* Racks, Current Magazines and Periodicals, for
   Reading rooms, for, 84-88
   Storage cases for, *see* Storage Cases, Periodicals, for
PETROLEUM LAMPS, 14
PIGEON-HOLES for sheaf catalogues, 99
PIPES—
   Distributing, 25
   Radiating, 23, 25
   Water, 28
   Weeping, 13
PLACARD CATALOGUES, 53
PLANNING, *see* Design of Public Libraries
PLATFORMS in lecture rooms, 101
"PLENUM" System of Ventilation, 24
POPULATION—
   Accommodation of library in relation to, 139, 140
   Number of branch libraries in relation to, 119
PORTER'S BOX, 105, 133
PRINT-CASES, 42, 43
PUBLIC LIBRARIES ACTS, *see under* Acts
PUBLIC ROOMS—
   Accessibility of, 127, 131
   Areas of, *see under* Areas
   Disposition of, 126, 131; uniformity of, 127, 128, 151
   Doors to, 10
   Height of, required for efficient ventilation, 22

R

RACKS—
   Current magazines and periodicals, for, 43, 44
   Newspaper files, for, 50
   Time-tables, for, 44

RADIATORS, position of, 23, 25, 26
RATE, LIBRARY, 114
   Effect of, on library organisation and building, 3
RATEPAYERS' READING ROOMS, 91
READERS—
   Accommodation for, *see* Reading Rooms
   Floor space for, 22, 81
   Table space required for, *see* Tables, Reading, Dimensions of
READING DESKS, *see* Tables, Reading
READING EASELS, *see* Easels, Reading
READING ROOMS, 81-91
   Areas required for, 22
   Chairs for, *see under* Chairs
   Disposition and spacing of furniture in, 81-84
   Juvenile, 89-91
   Lighting of, *see under* Lighting
   Periodicals, for—
     General periodical reading rooms, 88
     Magazine reading rooms, 87
       Combination of, with reference reading room, 98
     Newspaper reading rooms, 84-87, 127, 142
     Position of, 130, 131
     Screens and partitions for, 126
   Ratepayers', 91
   Reference, *see* Reference Department
   Students', 91, 98
   Women's, 88 ; position of, 113
READING SLOPES, disposition and spacing of, 84-86 ; *see also* Newspaper Reading Slopes
READING TABLES, *see* Tables, Reading
RECEIVING ROOMS, 107, 108
REFERENCE BOOKS in branch libraries, 150
REFERENCE DEPARTMENT, 92-98
   Barrier reference libraries, 92-95
     Catalogues in, 93
     Stack system in connection with, 93
     Tables (reading) in, arrangement of, 93
   Central library, in, 147
   Counters in, *see under* Counters
   Library systems, in, 146, 147
   Magazine room combined with, 98
   Open shelf reference libraries, 95-97
     Bookcases in, arrangement of, 95, 96, 97
     Catalogues in, arrangement of, 96, 97
     Students' tables in book room, 97
     Tables (reading) in, arrangement of, 96
     Wickets in, 96
   Reading rooms, position of, 126, 128, 131

REFERENCE DEPARTMENT (*continued*)—
   Reading tables for, *see under* Tables, Reading
   Rooms for special subjects and collections, 97, 98
   Students' reading rooms, 98
REFRESHMENT ROOMS, 103
RESIDENCES, librarians' *and* caretakers', *see under* Staff, Accommodation for
REVOLVING BOOKCASES, 39
ROLLING CASES, *see under* Bookcases
ROOF LIGHTS, 13
   Binderies, for, 107
   Disposition of building as affecting, 126
ROOFS, materials and construction of, 8

S

SAFE, librarian's room, for, 109
SCREENS, *see* Partitions
SEATS, *see* Chairs
SHEAF CATALOGUES, *see under* Catalogues
SHELVING, *see* Bookcases
SHOOT—
   Coals, for, 112
   Packing cases, for, 107, 108
SHOW-CASES FOR BOOKS, *see under* Bookcases
SHUTTERS, fireproof, 125
SILLS, WINDOW, *see under* Windows
SINKS, cleaners', 112
SITES—
   Gift of, 116
   Loans for, 116, 154
   Position of, 118, 119
   Purchase of, 116, 156
   Requirements of, 117-119
SKYLIGHTS, *see* Roof Lights
SLOPES, NEWSPAPER READING, *see* Newspaper Reading Slopes
SMOKING ROOMS, 101, 102
SOUND-PROOF CONSTRUCTION—
   Concert rooms, for, 102
   Floors, for, 7
   Walls, for, 7
SPARE ROOMS, 101, 102
SPEAKING-TUBES, 28
STACKS, *see* Book Stacks
STAFF—
   Accommodation for, 106-113
     Binderies, 107
     Branch libraries, in, 150
     Caretaker's residence, 110, 111, 143 ; position of, 126

STAFF (*continued*)—
  Accommodation for (*continued*)—
    Cataloguing rooms, 107
    Central libraries, in, 149
    Disposition of, 131-134
    Lending libraries, in,—
      Barrier system, 71, 75
      Open shelf system, 77, 78, 79
    Librarian's residence, 110, 111; position of, 126, 143
    Librarian's room, 108, 109
      Fittings and furniture in, 107
      Lavatory and closet in connection with, 109
      Outer office to, 108
      Position of, 108, 133
      Requirements of, 109
    Mess-rooms, 110
    Receiving and packing rooms, 107
    Workrooms, 106, 107
  Closets for, *see under* Closets
  Entrances for, 112, 113
  Lavatories for, *see under* Lavatories
  Rooms for, floors of, 6
  Small libraries, in, 142
  Staircases for, 112, 113

STAIRS—
  Book stacks, in, 66, 67
  Children's rooms, to, 89
  Dimensions of, requirements of London Building Act as to, 8, 9
  Materials for, 9
  Public, 8, 9, 105
  Staff, for, 112, 113

STANDS—
  Directory, 44
    Reference libraries, in,—
      Barrier system, 93
      Open shelf system, 96
  Newspaper files for reading rooms, for, 50

STEP-LADDERS, *see* Ladders

STEPS—
  Bookcases, for, *see under* Bookcases

STORAGE CASES—
  Books, for, 38, 39
  Periodicals, for, 43

STORE-ROOMS, 108
  Books, for, *see* Book Stores
  Periodicals, for, 69

STOVES, 25
  Binderies, for, 107
  Workrooms, in, 106

STRONG-ROOMS, 110

STUDENTS—
  Reading rooms for, *see under* Reference Department, *and* Reading Rooms
  Tables for, in book rooms, *see under* Book Rooms

STUDIES, 95, 98

SUPERVISION, 132-134
  Assisted by glazed screens, 59
  Disposition of bookcases to facilitate, 63, 64
  Misconceptions of, 108, 109
  Rooms for special subjects and collections, of, 97, 98

T

TABLES—
  Reading, 44-48
    Accessories, for 45, 48
    Children's rooms, in, 90, 91
    Construction of, 44, 45, 47
    Dimensions of, 44, 45, 47, 48, 90
    Disposition of, in reading rooms, 82, 83
    Magazine readers, for, 45, 46, 47, 87
    Materials for, 44
    Reference department, in, *see under* Reference Department
    Reference readers, for, 48
  Trestle, for workrooms, 106

TELEPHONES, 28, 105

THERMOMETERS, 26

TICKETS—
  Book, 57
  Borrowers', 57

TILE-LININGS, 7, 8

TIME-TABLES, racks for, *see under* Racks

TOBIN TUBES, 23

TONKS' FITTINGS, 37, 38

TOP LIGHTS, *see* Roof Lights

TRAVELLING LIBRARIES, 119

TRAYS—
  Borrowers' vouchers, for, 57
  Card-charging, for, *see under* Charging Appliances, Card

TREADLE LATCHES, 59
  Lending libraries (open shelf), in, 77
  Reference libraries, for, 96

TURNSTILES, 10

U

UMBRELLA CLIPS for chairs, 51

UMBRELLA STANDS, 60

V

VENTILATION, 21-24
  Areas required for efficient, 22
  Artificial, 22
  Book stores, of, 69
  Height of rooms required for efficient, 22
  " Plenum " system of, 24
  Store-rooms, of, 69
VESTIBULES, PUBLIC, 104, 105, 127 ; floors of, 6

W

WALLS—
  Internal—
    Omission of, in branch libraries, 134, 151
    Treatment of, 7, 8
      Colour, 13
      Dado in public rooms, colour of, 13 ; materials for, 7, 8
  Materials and construction of, 7, 8
  See also Partitions

WASTE PAPER—
  Bins for, 60, 112
  Boxes and baskets for, 60
WATER SUPPLY, 28
  Binderies, for, 107
  Expenditure on, 115
WICKETS, 10, 58-59, 96
  Lending libraries (open shelf system), in, 77, 78, 79
  Reference libraries, in, 96
  Treadle latches for, 59
WINDOWS, 10-13
  Book rooms, in, 62, 63
  Book stacks, in, 67
  Lending libraries, in, 80
  Outlook of, 124
  Sills of, height of, 12 ; in newspaper reading rooms, 85
WOMEN, special accommodation for, *see under* Reading Rooms
WOODWORK—
  Bookcases, in, 30, 31
  External, 8
  Fittings and furniture, in, 42
WORKROOMS, 106, 107

www.ingramcontent.com/pod-product-compliance
Lightning Source LLC
Chambersburg PA
CBHW080920180426
43192CB00040B/2569